What teenage girls don't tell their parents

Rich in practical tips, as well as providing some much needed humour and 'ah ha' moments. I've already added some of Michelle's parenting tips into my own repertoire and found them to work brilliantly!

                        Jen Hunter — Social Worker/Parent of teenage daughter

Michelle has a marvellous way of speaking the truth in a way that parents can all appreciate. Sometimes shocking, yet straight from the heart — an insightful read. Parents will benefit greatly from this book and find that they are not alone in their battle.

                        Dale Dearman — Guidance Officer/
                        Student Counsellor, Grace Lutheran College

Pity my mum's reading this — it just ruined all my future plans. Now I won't be able to get away with anything. Just kidding! This book is really good, and hits close to home. It will help us heaps.

                        Kate — 14 years old

What teenage girls don't tell their parents

Michelle Mitchell

First published in 2011
Australian Academic Press
32 Jeays Street
Bowen Hills Qld 4006
Australia
www.australianacademicpress.com.au

Copyright © 2011 text: Michelle Mitchell
Copyright © 2011 other contributions as indicated in the text: Australian Academic Press

Copying for educational purposes

The *Australian Copyright Act 1968* (Cwlth) allows a maximum of one chapter or 10% of this book, whichever is the greater, to be reproduced and/or communicated by any educational institution for its educational purposes provided that the educational institution (or the body that administers it) has given a remuneration notice to Copyright Agency Limited (CAL) under the Act.

For details of the CAL licence for educational institutions contact:
Copyright Agency Limited, 19/157 Liverpool Street, Sydney, NSW 2000.
E-mail info@copyright.com.au

Production and communication for other purposes

Except as permitted under the Act, for example a fair dealing for the purposes of study, research, criticism or review, no part of this book may be reproduced, stored in a retrieval system, or transmitted in any form or by any means electronic, mechanical, photocopying, recording or otherwise without prior written permission of the copyright holder.

National Library of Australia Cataloguing-in-Publication entry:

Author:	Mitchell, Michelle.
Title:	What teenage girls don't tell their parents / Michelle Mitchell.
ISBN:	9781921513770 (pbk.)
	9781921513787 (epub)
Subjects:	Teenage girls--Psychology.
	Parent and teenager.
Dewey Number:	305.2352

Cover illustration by Adriana Biaggini.
Photograph and cover design by Maria Biaggini.
Typeset in Garamond 12.5 pt by Australian Academic Press.

Foreword

Parenting teenage girls can be a daunting task, which at times requires seemingly saint-like degrees of patience. One of the major difficulties parents face is gauging the balance between overprotection and negligence, as well as determining when and how to intervene in their teen's life. With the advent of new communication technologies, including smart phones and mobile internet, teenagers are enjoying an increasing amount of freedom, autonomy, independence and perceived privacy from their parents. It is becoming much more difficult for parents to keep up to date with their teenagers' lives. Social networking has taken the world by storm. Some teenage girls eagerly broadcast their most precious secrets on the World Wide Web before sharing with their families. With reports of teen substance use and abuse, school truancy, high-risk sexual behaviours, depression and even suicide, parents have very real cause for concern.

Yet one of the common barriers to parent–teen communication is embarrassment about discussing these concerns (on both the parent and the teen's behalf). There can also be denial, confusion and an expectation that the problem will work itself out. Teens often adhere to the advice of their friends over their parents. While teens may struggle to believe their parents can relate to what they are going through, parents are typically slow to acknowledge the significant changes to society in recent decades. With incompatible expectations, communication breaks down.

The teen years are some of the most significant in terms of emotional, physical, behavioural, sexual and even spiritual development throughout one's lifetime. While their brain and body continue to form into the person they will spend the rest of their lives being, it is crucial that teenagers are provided with a consistent, positive guide for these years. Parental support is necessary to comfort, guide, protect, correct, encourage, mould and enjoy these years. Research has shown that being in a supportive family who use open communication to deal with problems can not only reduce the risk of high-risk harmful behaviours during this time, but also promote self-worth and emotional resiliency.

What Teenage Girls Don't Tell Their Parents is a refreshingly thoughtful take on the teenage girl's experience 'straight from the horse's mouth'. While at times humorous and at other times heartbreaking, Michelle Mitchell details the open and transparent experiences of teenage girls as they relate to parents and peers, providing the reader with insight into the collective mind of the adolescent female. The girls in this book could be any teenage girls; they could even be your own daughters. In a society that often looks at this young population with some disdain, each girl represented in this book is viewed as someone's precious daughter. This refreshing viewpoint delves beyond the surface complaints that teens often present with, to a deeper 'heart-level' connection, and sheds light on what our daughters are *really* thinking about. This is an unprecedented way for parents to take a glimpse inside their daughters' minds and to hear some of the secrets that they don't (but really do) want their parents to know, *before* their situation gets out of control. *What Teenage Girls Don't Tell Their Parents* provides practical advice in separating 'ordinary' teenage behaviour from behaviours that may warrant professional help. Guidance is also offered for the many tricky circumstances parents and daughters are likely to face throughout the teen years, helping mums and dads to view the present with more understanding so as to provide greater hope for their daughter's future.

Dr Robi Sonderegger
Humanitarian Activist & Clinical Psychologist

Contents

Foreword vii

Before we begin ... 1

What to expect in this book 5

Chapter One 9
Never judge a book by its cover

✿

Chapter Two 19
Did I say I hate you?
I really do love you

✿

Chapter Three 37
I don't care what you think!
I want your approval

✿

Chapter Four 59
She's my best friend forever
I want to be treated better

✿

Chapter Five   **85**

Why don't you trust me?
I want you to protect me

✿

Chapter Six   **105**

I have nothing to wear
I want to feel beautiful

✿

Chapter Seven   **129**

No one understands what I'm going through
I need help to deal with the pain

✿

Chapter Eight   **151**

It's all your fault
I know I can't blame you

✿

Conclusion   **169**

✿

Before we begin …

Scattered throughout this book are contributions by teenage girls aged between 13 and 17 years of age told in their own words. Each of these girls is a very 'normal' teenager, attending private or state high schools throughout Brisbane, Australia, where I work. They are very much like your daughter and her circle of friends.

If I were to read these stories and diary entries without knowing the teenagers who wrote them, I would assume that some of them were extremely troubled kids. I would also assume that they had parents who didn't care about them or the challenges they faced. However, I can assure you that all of the teenagers who contributed to this book belong to families who are very committed to them.

Their vital contributions to this book are a realistic picture of the issues and language of regular teenagers. None of them are made up or exaggerated. They are not written by out of control teenagers sliding into the juvenile justice system. In fact, each story is so common I could find hundreds of girls in similar situations in any local school, any day of the week.

I asked each teenager to write honestly, without restraint, explaining those things they chose not to say to their parents. In order to encourage transparency, they were told that none of their letters or diary entries would go straight to their parents or teachers. They understood that they would be published anonymously in order to protect their identity and the backlash they may understandably receive!

I was often surprised at how insightful their journals were and how articulately they expressed themselves. Many times their level of maturity far outweighed my expectations of them. Other times I cringed at their lack of maturity and the language they chose to use! In these cases I struggled to know whether to adjust their writing in order to make them more adult friendly. In the end, I opted to print the raw, untampered version that I believe best depicts the reality of their lives.

I want to say a big thank you to all the teenagers who were a part of creating this book. I had a great deal of fun working with you all. I enjoyed the challenge of giving your thoughts a clearer voice in the adult world. Thank you also to the parents who willingly allowed their daughters to be

Before we begin ...

involved. My hope is that your honesty will help families better understand and support their daughters as they grow into mature young women.

Michelle Mitchell
www.michellemitchell.org

What to expect in this book

I remember sitting in my hospital bed, having given birth to a baby just a few days before. Lying on the end of my bed was a huge pile of information. Some was from hospital staff, some from my friends, and some I had brought with me to read in my spare time. I obviously had no idea! There was undeniably some safety in being equipped for what felt like a daunting job. Just the fact that I had critical information lying on the end of the bed was empowering in itself.

Parents giving birth to a new baby always have a barrage of information presented to them. Information is offered from a range of professionals and is available at doctor's surgeries, hospitals, child care centres and baby clinics. There are books, websites and support groups; not to mention an ongoing flow of opinions from family and friends.

Although not all information new parents receive is right for their situation, they tend to take on board what is most relevant for them at that time. The best part about all this information is that parents are constantly presented with options. And these options always create opportunities for self-assessment, change and growth.

Parents often tell me that as their child has grown into a teenager, the amount of resources accessible to them has dwindled. Instead of being given information from all directions, parents feel like they have to hunt for it like a needle in a haystack. Parents of teenagers still need outside information to stimulate their personal growth and learning. Without such constant input, parents are unsure if what they are going through is normal.

In my experience, parents are reluctant to access counsellors or psychologists until things become critical. They are also rarely looking for a weekend seminar on 'how to be a great parent' as they find it both impersonal and difficult to fit into their already jam-packed schedule. My hope is that reading this book will provide a much needed alternative for you.

This book contains secrets that your teenager is only likely to tell you when they are much older. It is my hope that revealing these secrets today will give you an advantage and help you stay connected to your child as they grow up. If heard ahead of time, they have the potential to impact your parenting decisions today.

What to expect in this book

When parents ask me for direct parenting advice I am very hesitant to offer too many black and white opinions. Advice has an expectation that there is one right way to do things. Unfortunately, there are not always simple answers to situations and parenting a teenager is not that straight forward. I prefer to talk through options, and there is always a range of them!

Some of the examples in this book may describe your teenager perfectly and others may be less relevant. I encourage you to take what you can and literally shelve the rest. Every teenager is different, as is every family. If nothing else I hope this book allows you the time out of your normal schedule to think through what is best for your teenager at this point in their development.

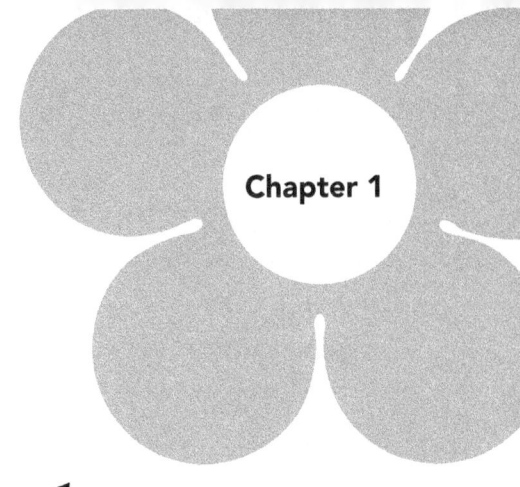

Chapter 1

Never judge a book by its cover

The teenage years

The inspiration for this book comes from many years of being at the coalface of mentoring teenage girls. I have literally been involved in thousands of teenagers and parents' stories, all which are as unique as they are complex. Each teenager I meet is someone's precious daughter. Most have a family who care deeply about them and the choices they are making. Each risk they take not only impacts their future, but the future of those whose life is entwined with theirs.

My guess is that you have picked up this book because you are totally committed to your child. You are committed in the way that all great parents are ... and there is no going back! My guess is that your 'child' is not just another teenager struggling to grow up. She is your daughter. That in itself makes her the most unique and important teenager in the world.

Young girls typically cross my path when they are between 13 and 15 years old. They are either attending or semi-attending high school, driving their parents insane and wanting to dress like they have just stepped out of a celebrity magazine. Their panic-stricken mums (some of the best mums I know panic a lot) usually explain the all-too-similar scenario, which goes something like this:

'I used to have a beautiful little girl who was so perfectly mannered and sweet. She was such a delight. Once she turned 13 she became a monster. She stopped talking to us. She won't do anything I tell her to do. We are fighting all the time. I don't feel like I can do anything right. I just don't know what went wrong. We love her so much but things are going from bad to worse.'

Once I speak with the teenage girls themselves, the story is usually the same.

Mega attitude

Smart mouth

I don't have any homework!

I can't live without the mobile phone

Teachers are evil — Parents just don't understand

My friends are the only people who really love me!

Get out of my room

Leave me alone

I just want to listen to my music

Tantrums and mood swings

I look soooooo fat in this size 6 dress!

Getting ready for school takes hours (and then a few more)

I have nothing to wear

Today was the worst day of my life

Withdrawn and depressed

It's your fault everyone hates me

Suspected binge drinking

Parents going grey

Why can't I have a boyfriend?

Father turning white

I am the only person not allowed to go to that party!

You can't stop me anyway

There is nothing wrong with my friends

It's not fair — No one understands

Why should I have to answer to you?

I can't wait until I can move out of home, after all I am nearly fifteen!

It is only after we talk through these important but quite surface subjects that something amazing happens. The mood of the conversation shifts and we begin to talk about the real issues. At this moment, young people choose to open the door to their highly private inner thoughts and feelings. They begin to speak honestly and from their heart, sometimes only for a few minutes, other times for hours. Simply put, I am privileged enough to be told their secrets.

I have always wanted to record these moments of genuine connection and give it to all the tired and discouraged mothers of the world. However, bound by confidentiality, no such recording could take place. My hands were tied and my lips were sealed. The insights I gained were unable to be repeated. I watched, in frustration, as teenagers' hearts closed at the same time their appointment ended.

Every chapter in this book focuses on a different secret I wished I could have told parents. Each chapter also uses real life examples, journal entries and letters from the teenagers who have revealed these secrets to me. Although you will be hearing their stories second-hand, I hope each teenager's words have the same impact on you as they had on me. I hope they empower your parenting and give you an added advantage when it comes to communicating with your teenager.

But before we get started, I want to explain where secrets come from.

It's what is inside that counts

I had a laugh the other day while I was scrolling through the Facebook pages of girls attending one of my small group programs. I saw the most glamorous photos and heard about the most incredible social lives. Quite frankly I couldn't believe I was reading about the same 15-year-olds I knew! I felt like I was scanning a celebrity's profile rather than a school girl's life! I didn't know whether to laugh or post a big fat sign on their page saying, 'Who is this phoney?'

Teenagers love the challenge of crafting an incredible Facebook page. It is their chance to be whoever they want to be. They can be exciting, attractive, popular, outrageous or even ten years older! They can, for a brief moment, live without the constraints of reality. They don't even have to tell the truth. In fact, the truth would really wreck things.

A teenager's Facebook page is simply who they want people to think that they are. But there is another side to every teenager. It is the side they choose not to post out to the world. What Facebook pages don't tell you is who a teenager is when there is no one around to impress. It doesn't tell you what they really think and feel about themselves when they are alone. It doesn't display their secret dreams, fears, flaws, immaturities and inconsistencies. And it never shows their pimples!

The saying, 'Never judge a book by its cover' is a great way to navigate through your teenager's Facebook page. No matter how your teenager appears on the surface I can absolutely guarantee that there is more to her than meets the eye. Her image is only the cover and title page of her life. There is a whole book under there!

I know that a lot of parents' time is spent worrying about their teenager's cover. It is important for parents to understand how fickle and unpredictable their teenager's cover can be. The cover that teenagers show can change dramatically depending on the circumstances they are in. They may use a rebellious cover when speaking to their parents and then use a sweet cover when answering their mobile phone! They may seem to be one person in front of their peers and a totally different person with their family.

A teenager's cover is simply their opportunity to look cool on their way to maturity, nothing more or less. A teenager's inside story however, is who they really are. Their inside story is based on authentic truth rather than fiction. It is highly valuable. It is far more difficult to get to know. It is really important that parents understand the difference between a teenager's external image and her internal world. Her internal world is where secrets come from.

How your teenager looks on the inside is as unique as how they look on the outside. No one else has exactly the same inside story as they do. Because of this, many teenagers wonder if anyone else will understand it. It becomes a highly personal and complex story to tell. It can be quite difficult for a teenager to express their inside story and they often assume they will be misunderstood or not listened to.

The biggest challenge that parents face is staying connected to their teenager's inside story. This is especially challenging when what screams the loudest and what demands the most immediate attention is their cover. What is really going on inside of a teenager doesn't always get communicated well or even at all.

I would never suggest that a parent ignore their teenager's cover, but I will say this: A cover can so easily distract parents. It can take them on an emotional roller-coaster that leaves them confused. A teenager's cover, with all its challenges, needs to be kept in perspective. When it becomes the sole focus of communication it is gaining too much attention.

The inside story and parenting

Picture the following scenario. Olivia's friend Amanda rings the home phone at about 7 pm. Amanda invites Olivia to a party she is having at her house on Saturday night. It is apparently going to be the best party ever and everyone is going to be there. Of course, Olivia promptly asks her mum, who in turn asks the usual questions — 'Will any adults be there? Who else is going? Can I speak to Amanda's mother?'

Olivia's mother didn't get the answers she was looking for, so she had to say no to her daughter. In normal teenage behaviour Olivia proceeded to 'hit the fan'.

She spent the next few hours dramatically whingeing about how unfair it was for her mother to say no to the most important social engagement on the Year 8 calendar. She called her mother a few choice words for not understanding how important this party was to her. After all, everyone would be there … everyone except her that is! She called her mother overprotective and strict for even asking to speak to Amanda's mother. Why would any parent in their right mind do that!

Olivia's poor mother went to bed feeling like she had gone three rounds in a boxing ring. She began to question whether in fact she was being too strict or unreasonable. After all, her daughter was now almost 13 and could be trusted to be responsible, couldn't she? In the early hours of the morning she even considered changing her mind and allowing her to go to the party after all.

A few days later the dust settled. I had my weekly appointment with Olivia and her mother. Olivia's mother was keen to discuss the incident. She hoped to have her actions supported as she was still second-guessing herself. I could tell she didn't quite know where to start in order to explain the tension that had escalated in her home.

Olivia took the initiative to relay the story. She was in a happy and chatty mood having come from a great day at school! She was now freely (and expressively) telling the whole story, rather than the version she had previously told her mother. She was obviously dying to tell someone! She simply opened her mouth and a waterfall of truth came out.

Her story went something like this ... 'Amanda asked me to the party but her mum wasn't going to be there. Amanda's brother's friend was bringing alcohol and Amanda was going to get drunk. Mum wanted to speak to Amanda's mum which would have wrecked EVERYTHING! I HAD to lie so mum wouldn't get on the phone because Amanda would have been REALLY mad at me. Inside I was really hoping that mum would say no. I didn't really want to go.'

Olivia's mum was totally shocked. And then I watched as shock turned into horror, and horror into anger. I could see the tops of her ears going red. If I hadn't been around I am sure Olivia would have been in big trouble!

'Why didn't you just tell me the truth? Why didn't you just tell me that you didn't want to go?' asked her mum in shock.

Olivia's answer didn't surprise me.

'I dunno,' she started. 'I knew you would say no. I didn't want to be rude to Amanda! She's my friend! No one really expected me to be there. I am always the one not allowed to go,' she complained.

'I wonder why?!' I thought to myself quietly.

Olivia's mum learnt a lot that day simply by hearing her daughter's secrets. I think the biggest eye-opener for her was not that there was going to be alcohol at Amanda's party or that her mum wouldn't be home. I think she intuitively guessed that. The biggest secret was that Olivia didn't really want to go to the party quite as much as she appeared to.

I believe if parents knew a few more of their teenager's inner thoughts, it would save them a lot of time worrying if they have done the right thing. It would also save them from being pressured into making decisions they weren't totally comfortable with. It would give them an advantage — just what every parent needs in order to maintain their confidence while parenting a teenage girl!

Chapter 2

Did I say I hate you?

I really do love you

Is this normal?

Like many parents you have probably spent the last 13 (or more) years deliberately investing in your child's development. From the moment they entered the world, parenting became your priority. You may have taken time off work, existed without sleep, laboriously supervised homework and monitored piano practice. You may not have been perfect, but you worked hard, understanding that your child needed you.

And then your child became a teenager! And not just any teenager — a teenage girl!

Parent's rarely know what to expect during the teenage years so they understandably cross their fingers and hope for the best. Although few parents would expect to see their teenager wake up at 13 'all grown up', they may hope to start seeing a responsible young lady emerge. They may hope to see progressive signs of maturity. Unfortunately, these hopes rarely unfold easily.

The teenage years often bring a regression in behaviour, when parents are expecting a progression. Most teenage girls produce more tantrums than a 2-year-old, give their parents more sleepless nights than a newborn baby, and have more mood swings than they could ever experience on a playground. And if parents are really lucky they might sometimes see brief glimmers of maturity!

I often hear parents say things like, 'She is supposed to know better.' 'She is supposed to be responsible.' 'She is not a child anymore and we should be able to trust her.' Theoretically you may be right. Development, like a good investment account, should be steadily moving forward. However, the reality is that your daughter is more likely to represent the ups and downs of a volatile stock market. There is nothing steady about most teenage girls.

There is a common misconception I have noticed among parents. This misconception is that as a child gets older, and gains more independence, parenting should become easier. In my experience, nothing is further from the truth. You can expect to find parenting a teenager the most time-consuming, challenging and draining stage of your life so far! You can expect to hear yourself say 'Who is that girl?' when you would prefer to be saying 'I am so proud of you'.

It is so important that parents get their expectations right, from the beginning. I can guarantee that if your child is in their formative teenage years, they need you now more than ever before. They need you more than when they relied on you to feed them, tie their shoe laces, cut their sandwiches or walk them across the street. If you consider having a teenager as intense as bringing a new baby home, then double it — you might be close to understanding the effort it will take to see them mature into an adult.

After 13 years it is very common for parents to feel tired and ready to 'let go'. I'd like to encourage you to hang in there a little longer, pull out the reserves and run the final leg of the race. Your teenager still needs you so much. It is not time to exit yet. If you need to readjust your thinking or your schedule, do so. It is too early to expect to see a young adult emerging — you have a teenager. There is a huge difference between the two.

The journey forward

A child's journey to adulthood can be divided into three distinct stages — dependence, independence and interdependence. Parents who have a realistic understanding of what to expect in each stage have a far better chance of dealing with each phase constructively.

STAGE 1: DEPENDENCE

In this stage babies and young children rely predominately on their parents. Parents are the sole providers of their basic needs including food, clothing, shelter and comfort. Parents also filter the external relationships and learning opportunities that shape their future.

In return, parents are appreciated in endless childlike ways. A warm hug, an excited smile when their dad comes home, an enthusiastic, 'I love this lasagne mum!' And although this stage is very physically draining it is also filled with the joy of seeing your child progress because of your input!

What to expect:
- a child-centred relationship
- lots of hard work
- physically tiring activities
- small rewards that make it all worthwhile
- the joy of seeing a child grow and develop.

STAGE 2: INDEPENDENCE

This stage of the journey can be seen lurking on the horizon for several years before it fully arrives. The first time your child slams the car door as they leave for school (and doesn't look back) you know things are on the move. Parents of 10-year-olds regularly tell me they are acting like teenagers already. I reassure them that there is more to come!

During this stage young people desire a 'life' independent of their parents. They are looking for their place outside of the security of their home. They often want to discover their own view of the world and are questioning what they have been taught by their parents. However, they lack the maturity and character to fully embrace independence. There is often a huge gap between what they want to do and what they have the maturity to handle. Many teenagers still seem to need guidance in order to ensure they eat well and sleep enough!

It is really easy to identify a teenager who is at this stage. They inhabit an atmosphere that says 'I don't need you' and display an attitude that says 'I already know it all'. They are repelling authority like it is the plague. One of the biggest shocks to parents is their ability to distance themselves from the advice, love and protection that they have previously embraced.

The independence stage appears in different degrees of expression and for different lengths of time. Some young people reach this stage later in their teenage years or even early twenties. Others pass it so quietly it is hardly noticed. I have found that when a young person reaches the stage of independence early in their teenage years, it usually hits hard. If your child is between 13 and 16 years of age in this stage of development, you will have your hands full.

It is easy to criticise, judge or even reject young people who are at this stage. However, I encourage parents to realise that this is a normal part of development. If teenagers feel 'wrong' for going through this developmental stage they can carry resentment and it can fuel their negative choices. Although the behaviour is not always right, the struggles and feelings are not wrong — they are a genuine part of growing up.

What to expect:
- a child-centred relationship
- an unpredictable, emotionally draining daily experience

- a challenge to your authority and opinions
- increased workload
- greater need for deliberate parenting
- little immediate reward, commonly leaving parents feeling inadequate and unappreciated.

STAGE 3: INTERDEPENDENCE

During this stage young people are able to consistently take care of their own basic needs and function in the adult world. That means they don't rely on their mum to wash their clothes and get them up in the morning. They are no longer expecting their parents to pay for their way in life. They have learnt how to take responsibility for their own wellbeing and future.

However, they also know that there are times when it is appropriate to reach out and ask for help. Real maturity comes when a young person is able to accept that they have an inner circle of people whose support they need. Interdependence describes a young person's ability to rely on their parents (and others who have proven their love for them) during the difficult times in their life. Young people in this stage realise that they have an impact on others and consider this carefully when making decisions.

Parents should be encouraged by the thought that interdependence is on the other side of independence. I have found that interdependence slowly develops over time. It is more likely to appear if the right support is available to teenagers during the independent stage.

What to expect:
- a two-way relationship
- a responsible adult who is able to care for her own basic needs
- a young person able to initiate communication and ask for advice
- the reward of seeing a young adult emerge.

'I want to be independent'

Dear Diary

My parents want to know everything. Mum even came into my room today. I can tell because stuff is moved and she puts things away where I can't find them. I don't want her anywhere near my stuff. It is NONE of her business. It is MY space and MY life and they should keep out. She makes me so mad when she thinks she can come in and just touch things. And I don't want her to clean my room ever. I have private stuff in here. I like it messy. It is the way I am. She might think it's a problem but I don't. Everyday they say, How was your day? What happened today? Like I want to tell them and have a big chat about stuff they just won't understand. What do they know about anything! They just check up on me all the time. I can't do anything! I can't wait until I can leave home and do whatever I want to do. I won't have anyone tell me what to do anymore. I want to make my own choices. They are constantly nagging me about my homework and they won't let me go out. They won't let me do anything like getting a piercing or having a boyfriend.

(continued over)

> They won't even let a boy talk to me for more than 10 minutes on the phone without dad saying 'Time to get off now'. And they breathe down my neck when I am on the internet like I am looking at porn or something. They don't trust me, which is stupid because I can take care of myself. No one else has parents like mine. They just don't get that I am grown-up and I don't need them hanging onto me like a baby anymore. They don't understand that I don't need them anymore. I can make up my own mind and make my own decisions. Like my dad will EVER be ok with that!
>
> **Katie, age 14**

Dear Diary

> I don't want to talk to my mum about things. She is a total b****. She is the last person in the world I want to talk to. I just wish she would leave me alone and get the f*** out of my life. I have nothing to say. Sometimes you can't talk to your parents like you can your friends. Like if you have a boyfriend and you say you are in love, they say you can't be because you are too young. I was going out with Beau and my mum hated him. She tried to put a restraining order on him which is totally weird. And she wonders why I don't want to talk to a freak! I can do whatever I want to because it's my f***** body and my life and she can't control what I do. If I want to drink alcohol that is my business! She just doesn't get that I don't need her anymore. It's time for her to back off and get out.
>
> **Jennifer, age 13**

> ## Dear Diary
>
> I can't breathe in this house. LITERALLY! I am suffocating! My parents just won't leave me alone. I can't do anything without them knowing. They watch me like a hawk with evil eyes! They want to control everything in my life! My mum put a lock on my computer because I was staying up till 2 am on it. Now I give her attitude because my computer locks me out when everyone gets on. It is on a stupid timer thing that I HATE! I get so so so so mad. I yell @ her. My dad said that if I didn't stop giving my mum attitude he would take the computer away. They are totally ridiculous. What am I going to do without the computer? It will only make things worse between us. *Get out of my life parents and leave me alone. That would make things better.*
>
> **From Meg, age 16**

The diary entries above typify the independent stage of a teenager's life. Anyone who has a daughter in this stage will recognise the demands for freedom, the cry for total independence and the undertone that says, 'Don't you dare tell me what to do!'

Take comfort — most young people in this stage sound very similar.

One of the biggest challenges for parents of teenagers is the feeling of being pushed out of their teenager's life. This is especially true when commonsense tells parents that they very much need to be involved. This power struggle is a common part of growing up. During this stage parents often vocalise feelings of rejection, some to the point of feeling hated by their child.

Because I spend a great deal of time mentoring teenage girls I often have mothers bring their daughters to me when they are at the end of their rope — exhausted and needing some urgent back-up! As I watch a daughter and her mother walking into my office, I see two individuals in quite different emotional states. Even before they open their mouths their body language communicates two different stories.

Teenage girls are commonly carrying their boxing gloves, ready for a fight and hating authority. They are aggressively maintaining the stance that they are right and in control of their own lives. On the other hand, mothers are visibly battered. Their expectations are shattered and they are usually feeling guilt-ridden, rejected, confused and desperate for answers. It never ceases to amaze me how much a teenager can make a grown woman feel inadequate, ugly, uninteresting … and that's all just before breakfast!

A few months ago one particular mother dragged her daughter to my office. When I say 'dragged', I mean literally dragged. Emily was far from happy about the experience. As her mother introduced herself and the situation, Emily busied herself by yawning, looking around the room and rolling her eyes. The more Emily refused to engage, the more disheartened her mother became. Finally her mother burst into tears and said, 'All I want is to have a relationship with her. She thinks I want to hurt her but I don't. She doesn't understand that I still have to be her mother. I only want the best for her. I just want her to be happy.'

Emily understood how powerful a weapon her love was. She knew she was literally holding her mother's heart in the palm of her hand, and she was using her attitude like a dagger. Emily defended herself by saying, 'She doesn't love me. If she loved me she would let me go out and actually do something! All she does is cry all the time and it is making my angry. She needs to get over it. I hate her and in two weeks I am 15 and she can't stop me leaving home!'

I braced myself and asked mum to give me some time alone with her delightful daughter!

After an hour or so of talking to Emily I asked her some pointed questions.

'Do you think your mother really loves you?'

Without flinching she looked at me as if I were an absolute idiot she replied, 'Of course she does.'

'How do you think she feels when you speak to her like that?'

'I guess she is pretty cut up … she cries a lot,' Emily answered.

(Get ready for it parents … SECRET TIME!)

'Emily, do you love your mum?'

With most teenagers I have found their immediate response to this situation is an embarrassed exclamation about expecting too much. Telling your mother, the one who carried you, put her life on hold, cries herself to sleep over you and is worried sick about you that you love them seems beyond comprehension!

Emily understandably paused.

She looked at the floor.

She began to fidget.

I knew the truth was about to come out. I knew she was going to tell me something she had been longing to get off her chest for a while.

'Yeah, I do. I mean I know I don't act like it but she is my mum. I just get angry and say bad stuff but I don't really mean it. I feel really bad for treating her like that. It makes me feel horrible because she loves me so much and would do anything for me and I treat her so bad. I am a total bitch! I don't know why I do it. I think about it all the time. Sometimes I lay awake at night feeling terrible about it.'

'Would you be willing to tell your mum the truth? Would you be willing to tell your mum you love her?' I asked hopefully.

'Yes, I think it would help us sort things out,' Emily replied.

I noticed a tear in her eye. (Breakthrough moment!)

I asked Emily's mum to enter the room again. I get ready to pull out the big one, the question that will unite the two of them forever.

'Emily you know your mum loves you,' I begin. 'I know you have said some pretty mean things to her, but underneath it all do you love her?'

Emily pauses.

Did I say I hate you?

Mum looks like she is going to pass out.

Emily's body tightens up as she and proudly announces, 'Sometimes, but only when she lets me go out!'

(Ahhhhhhhhhhhhhh! SOMETIMES! SOMETIMES!) I wanted to kill her! Why couldn't she have just said what she said to me moments before! Now I have a problem on my hands. Mum's eyes well up with tears again. I can see her thinking, 'My daughter really hates me!' But there could be nothing further from the actual truth.

Emily smiles, then catches my eye and looks down.

Emily understands that both giving and withholding love is a powerful weapon in relationships. And in order for Emily's mother to remain an active parent she needs to know Emily's secret. She needs to know that at the bottom of Emily's heart is a great love and respect for her mother. This will change her parenting forever.

This story may seem a bit over the top for your household, or maybe not. But most mothers and fathers feel redundant at some stage as their teenager bucks for their independence. It is amazing how similar the words 'Get out of my life', 'I don't need your opinion' or 'You can't tell me what to do anyway!' can sound like 'I hate you' to parents who are wanting to connect with their daughter.

Your teenager is unlikely to wave a 'Mum's the best' fan club flag for some years yet. They aren't going to sing your praises voluntarily, so you have to *know it* rather than rely on being told (or experiencing) it. You have to remind yourself every day that they love you, even when they are fighting with you or hurling abuse. You have to remind yourself that you know their secret!

If you believe the message of rejection your teenager is sending you, you are greatly mistaken. This mistake will rob you of your ability to be the parent they need you to be — one who is sure and confident that they are still very much needed and valued as part of their child's life.

The sacrificial investment

You can't build your relationship with your teenage daughter on bribes, nor can you build your relationship on control, and you certainly can't build it on keeping score.

Love is the only foundation for a parent–child relationship. Love is the only thing that will overlook faults, suffer long, and bear pain. Love is what will eventually get you through your differences. A relationship that is founded on love will stand the test of time and outlast any temporary challenges.

The real challenge for parents however, is that teenagers demand unconditional love but seldom give it. They expect you to be faultless, able to give and give and give, listen and listen and listen. They expect you to endure getting emotionally dumped on and then continue parenting with a smile as if nothing has happened. They expect you to keep up with the intensely changing pace of emotion they throw out and stay stable through it.

To teenagers, a relationship with their parents is a one-way street. And not surprisingly the destination is centred on them. I have rarely met a teenager who doesn't expect their parents to place their interests, needs and emotions as a priority. For parents, the journey of parenting a teenager is long and they may feel like there is no end in sight.

Does this sound familiar? 'I hate you *but* ...'
'Can you drive me to Emma's house?'
'Can I have $10 to go to the movies?'
'Can you cook me dinner before I go out?'
'Can you buy me new shoes?'
'Can you wash my uniform for tomorrow?'
'Can I have your car when I get my license?'
(And now for the BIG ONE):
'I hate you but I expect you to love me!'

It is difficult to love when there is nothing coming back in return. You have the incredible challenge of being the adult, staying the adult, and loving unconditionally regardless of what your child throws at you.

Parents therefore need to be prepared to make a sacrificial investment into their child's life. This investment can't be replaced by someone else's input. This investment is costly, draining, demanding, annoying and testing to say the least.

I see such a dramatic difference in those young people who are privileged enough to have a relationship that offers them this. Providing unconditional and consistent love is probably the most important gift you can give your teenager. When you offer your teenager unconditional love, it enables them to feel safe. They know they don't have to earn your love or perform to be accepted. They have the security of knowing that there is one person who is always fighting for them.

Teenagers look intently for this type of love, especially when they feel unlovely (which all do at some stage!). It is natural for teenagers to look outside of their home for this acceptance and belonging. This doesn't mean parents aren't providing enough love for them. It does, however, mean that parents need to be even more diligent in reinforcing that they are the safe place that their teenager is looking for.

I encourage parents to communicate their love for their teenager deliberately. Once a year is not enough! Once a month is not enough! Do it everyday … regardless of how they are responding to you. Don't wait for the big, deep and meaningful discussion to communicate to your teenager that you love them. What stays with them the most is what is communicated to them on a daily basis.

Yes, I can hear what you are thinking, 'They don't deserve it. When I reach out they reject me.' The fact is that you are probably right. However, your love for your child is not a reward but a given. It is on offer regardless of how they respond to you. If you ration your love according to whether they show their love for you, you will have a disaster on your hands. They need your love, despite how hurtful their behaviour is.

This presents the challenge of being able to love without expecting an immediate return. Even if your teenager is behaving in the most inappropriate ways, remember that unconditional love never fails. You can do many things wrong as a parent, but you can't afford not to transfer your love for them each time they reach out for it (and even when they don't). Your love for them is the only thing they will remember and it is how they judge your worth as a parent.

Remember that every teenager needs to be loved. Your teenager wants to discover how much you love them and goes to endless measures to test that love. Parents need to recognise that during each interaction, no matter where or when it takes place, your teenager is looking for reassurance that you love them. They are presenting you with the same question over and over again — 'Will you love me even if I don't show love to you?' How you react to that question can have serious consequences.

Isabella was a part of a girl's group I ran this year. On a weekly basis she would tell me about the fights she was having with her mum. Things seemed to be escalating at an alarming pace. It was obvious that her behaviour was more than challenging her mother's patience. In a moment of anger her mother told her daughter she wanted to send her to a foster home. Now I don't believe for a minute that she really meant it. However, her mum was feeling so unloved by Isabella that she wanted to wipe the sight of her. (Sound familiar?) This was a damaging turning point in their relationship. It opened the door for Isabella to leave home and stay with friends for weeks at a time. It opened the door for unsupervised time that soon involved drug use. Teenagers are looking for the opportunity to say, 'See, she doesn't love me anyway! It doesn't matter if I do what I want.' Your teenager needs to know that regardless of the challenges she is presenting, the door is never shut.

No one in the world will ever be able to replace your role in your daughter's life. Not her friends. Not her future husband. Not her own children. Not another human being, ever. You are the only parent or primary carer she will ever have. That means that you can offer her a relationship that eventually she won't be able to say no to.

I can guarantee that when she is alone she wonders how you are coping with her attitude. She wonders how you are putting up with her. She wonders why you are continuing to reach out to her, in spite of how horrible she is being. This is the best type of wondering she can do — it is the wonder that great parenting is meshed in.

Chapter 3

I don't care what you think!

I want your approval

How much attention does this girl need!

Belinda is finally ready to go out to the movies with her friends. She has spent hours putting the right outfit together and excitedly comes down to ask her family the big question, 'How do I look?'

'You look lovely,' mum responds, graciously ignoring the layers of jet-black eyeliner!

Dad is busy finishing his coffee but tries to look interested. He is quite oblivious to the time and effort she has invested, so instead of complimenting her, he takes the practical route.

'You might want to take a jumper,' he says. 'It might be cold outside.'

Horrified that her father didn't notice she was the picture of perfection, Belinda stormed upstairs to get a jumper. Dad notices she is getting madder and madder with every step. She finally slams the door and yells, 'I don't care what you think anyway!' Her dad and brother look at each other and crack up laughing, unsure of what else to do. They are totally unaware of Belinda's deep need for their approval. The last thing they heard is that she doesn't even care!

It is usually in absolute exasperation that fathers ask me the question: 'How much attention does this girl need? I mean seriously! We tell her we love her all the time. We drive her everywhere. We take good care of her. We listen to her go on and on and on and then I make one little suggestion, like you might want to get a jumper ... and suddenly it's "You don't love me, you don't care about me, you think I am a baby, you don't trust me!" I just want to be able to speak to her normally!'

A teenage girl's bottomless need for approval is often difficult for them to articulate, and challenging for parents to understand. It seems that no matter how much you love them, they always need more. No matter how much you praise them, they just can't get enough. It's like each second needs its own compliment. Like each hour needs its own fanfare. Quite frankly, parents — especially dads — find it exhausting!

For most adults, receiving another's approval is a pleasant experience. It is an enjoyable and valued part of their lives. Not so for teenagers! For teenage girls, approval is such a dominant need it can literally run their lives. It is often the first thing on their mind when they get up in the morning and the last thing on their mind when they go to sleep at night. It can override any small ounce of logic they possess at any time it chooses! Teenagers thrive on it and can't survive without it.

A teenager's need for approval is so foundational that it has a strong impact on the decisions they make every day. Teenagers regularly consider whether their actions will be approved or disapproved of by their peers. They not only consider whether they will be approved of but carefully weigh the implications associated with this perception.

If you think your teenager is stronger than that, think again. Most errors in judgment, where a teenager has acted out of character, can be traced back to an overriding need for acceptance and approval. I have seen occasions when this desire for approval has literally meant the difference between life and death.

Parents, ask yourself:
- Is your daughter able to handle being ridiculed by her peers?
- Is she confident enough to stand against the tide of common opinion?
- Is she secure enough to know her value under pressure?

You may feel that you should be answering 'yes' to these questions when in fact I hope you answered 'no'. No is the realistic answer to these questions in the light of teenagers' maturity.

Should you be concerned?

The issue here is really about self-esteem. So let's look at what self-esteem is.

A person who has positive self-esteem has the ability to like and feel good about themselves, regardless of what circumstances they find themselves in. Every adult's self-esteem can fluctuate. However, people who have a strong self-image will be less likely to develop negative feelings about themselves, and far less likely to maintain those feelings over a period of time.

In order to maintain a consistent level of positive self-esteem that is able to bounce back after difficult times in life, a person needs to understand their intrinsic value. They need to have a solid appreciation of their strengths and be able to approach their weaknesses — knowing that some things can be changed, while others need to be graciously accepted. People with strong self-esteem don't love everything about themselves. They simply embrace the idea that they are a valuable human being.

I don't know about you, but I think the ability to do this is totally unrealistic for most 14-year-olds. That might sound a bit harsh, but let me explain. A positive, consistently strong, resilient self-esteem is founded on a particular perspective. This type of perspective understands that everyone has weaknesses and that life isn't perfect. It understands mature concepts such as 'everything has a purpose' and 'every cloud has a silver lining'. A perspective like this usually only comes with life experience, maturity and time. A teenager's self-esteem will always lack this.

I am not suggesting that teenagers can't feel good about themselves. They often do. However, they also often feel very bad about themselves and find it difficult to rationally bring the way they think about themselves back into balance. They also find it difficult to separate who they are from what they do, or others' opinions of what they do.

Most parents are not expecting their daughter to be the most confident girl in school. What they do want is to know that she is on the road to developing the confidence she will need to pursue her dreams and overcome challenges. They want to know that she will be able to cope well with life. In order to help them make this assessment, most parents quietly compare how their daughter's confidence stacks up against others her own age.

To help you in this process (and save you from snooping around and asking your daughter's friends indirect but loaded questions) I have put together a list of things that parents either should or shouldn't be alarmed about. This list is based on my observation of teenage girls over the past 15 years. It hasn't changed much over time and remains a list of guidelines I keep coming back to.

DON'T be concerned if she struggles with her confidence …

How confident would you feel if you had a face full of pimples and a bucket-load of new hormones? There is so much change going on in (and around) teenagers that it isn't always realistic for them to feel secure. They are transitioning to another season in life. They are often still deciding whether they like the grown-up version of themselves. In my opinion, it is totally understandable that they are not always confident.

DON'T be concerned if every day is different ...

A teenager's self-esteem can change dramatically from day to day and even moment to moment. They can be on top of the world one day and in the depths of despair the next. One day they can think they are the funniest, most beautiful and popular person in the school. The next day they can think they are the most ugly, unwanted, unlovable person ever created. And although how you feel about yourself is subject to change, teenagers take it to a whole new level! Teenagers live in the here and now; their self-esteem is limited to that moment. How they feel about themselves 'now' is what clouds their judgment and limits their perspective.

DON'T be concerned if she uses extreme language ...

'I hate my hair!' 'I am so dumb!' These are just some of the extreme words teenagers may use to describe themselves. I speak to hundreds of teenage girls a year and most of them would openly say they dislike themselves or at least a good part of themselves. Understandably, it is the way in which they say they dislike themselves that alarms many parents. Your teenager may find the most extreme language possible to express their disappointment with themselves. By nature teenagers exaggerate, especially in front of their peers. Most of them, however, will ditch the extreme language as they mature.

DON'T be concerned if she thrives on praise ...

I have never seen a teenage girl who wasn't obsessed with others' opinions about her. For most girls, being accepted is their number one priority. It either makes or breaks their entire day. Don't be worried if your teenager looks for praise and approval in order to lift her mood. They are often simply discovering that attention feels good.

DON'T be concerned if she is still developing realistic expectations ...

It is not uncommon for teenagers to think that feeling 'on top of the world', 'being the centre of attention' or 'having everyone like them all the time' is normal. As a result, they can feel rejected when they come in second place, or feel down if they weren't the best dressed, or an utter failure if they didn't get noticed. They are getting used to disappointment and learning that it doesn't have to rock their world. Teenagers haven't yet had enough experience to accept that life and friendships have highs and lows.

DO be concerned if she is always down ...

There are always a few girls whose self-esteem stands out as being a concern. These are girls who are stuck in a negative perspective of themselves and their lives. Their negative feelings rarely change, regardless of which environment they are in. Their perspective is difficult to shift and takes a great deal of effort to marginally improve.

Symptoms
- feeling negative about herself most of the time
- mood only lifts marginally
- feeling that their life is not worth living
- finding it difficult to like herself and enjoy life.

Mindsets to learn
- life is meant to be enjoyed
- it is ok to like yourself
- every person has weaknesses.

If you feel that your daughter is getting stuck in a negative mindset and is becoming depressed you should seek professional support from a qualified psychologist.

DO be concerned if she constantly strives for perfection …

Very early in life children learn that doing a job well means increased approval. When teenagers begin to take this one step further and associate perfection with ultimate approval, they gear themselves up for constantly feeling negative about themselves. They are chasing perfection, which isn't attainable and won't reward them for their efforts in the way they hope. Teenagers can easily learn how to control the amount of attention and approval they receive by altering themselves. Again, remember that all teenagers do this to some degree, but when it is a driving force that overrides their enjoyment of life it becomes a concern.

Symptoms
- looking down on people who aren't striving for the same perfection
- continually driving herself to be the best
- falling apart if she can't win or be in control.

Mindsets to learn
- people enjoy being around someone who is happy rather than someone who is always striving for approval or attention
- trying to earn people's approval usually backfires and repels people
- people value a range of internal attributes (faithfulness, kindness) just as much as external attributes (appearance, possessions)
- you have to know what is valuable about you as a person so you can offer it to others.

DO be concerned if she can't say 'no' ...

Teenagers with poor self-esteem may find it difficult to voice their own opinions and say 'no' to others. They may find themselves saying 'yes' in order to avoid offending or disappointing someone whose approval they desire. Their priority is pleasing people and looking good at all costs. If this is your teenager, don't panic but realise that their self-esteem will need to be nurtured a little longer. Make special note that they will be more heavily reliant on external approval while their concept of themselves is developing. Also realise that their current state of mind could lead them to make choices they will later regret.

Symptoms

- looking to others' opinions before voicing her own
- making 'out of character' decisions when pressured by others
- putting others' needs and ideas before her own.

Mindsets to learn

- saying 'no' takes practice
- saying 'no' may initially feel uncomfortable
- the consequences of saying 'no' are usually far less than you imagine
- you are valuable and worth protecting
- when you are confident people have confidence in you.

DO be concerned if she is entrenched in a popular culture of poor self-esteem ...

Having poor self-esteem has become a popular part of teen culture in recent years. The rise in depression, self-hatred and self-harm has set a new benchmark in what is perceived as normal teenage behaviour. Because of this, there is greater potential for teenagers to embrace patterns of behaviour that will limit their future potential. Poor self-esteem may stop a teenager from trying, caring, being happy and experiencing life. There is nothing sadder than seeing a teenager embrace low self-esteem because it is popular and accepted by their peers.

Symptoms
- gravitating to the negative side of life (death, harm, evil)
- deliberately rejecting things associated with happiness.

What to do
- seek professional help if there are signs of depression
- treat talk about death or suicide seriously
- introduce and/or maintain as many positives as possible
- maintain normal routines (school, sensible eating)
- eliminate as many negatives as possible
- monitor what is watched and listened to on television, movies, internet, and music.

Making/breaking confidence

While it might never happen in your household, for those who are honest enough to say you don't have it all together the following story is for you. I like to call it the psycho-parent moment. It is a 'I was tired to start with, I've had enough for one day and I'm losing my mind' blow-out moment!

The evening's disagreement started with a relatively simple issue. Emily's mother had found an English assignment sheet in the bottom of her bag, scrunched around an old banana skin and an empty yoghurt container. To her shock the due date was *tomorrow*! It was absolute panic for her mother but for Emily, well, what's the big deal? She had it under control. After all it was only 9 pm and she had 10 hours before she left for school the next day! No sweat!

Within minutes emotions went from 1 to 110, and before too long Emily and her mum were screaming blue murder at each other. By the end of the night one issue had led to another and the argument now involved everything Emily had done wrong in the last 12 months. Poor mum had become exasperated and was flapping around like a chook with its head cut off. She called Emily lazy, disrespectful, a liar, untrustworthy and a shame to the family. She even went so far as to say she wondered if Emily would ever amount to anything.

And Emily wasn't taking it lying down! In true teenage style she was adding fuel to the fire by calling her mother a stupid cow, control freak, homework maniac and some other choice words that we can leave to the imagination. The situation was a mess! Mum's heated emotions meeting a stubborn child's defiance — a bad combination.

The final blow came when Emily made sure she knew that her mother's opinion of her meant nothing. Emily made it quite clear that she didn't care (and never will care) what her mother thinks of her. Full stop!

With that it was over for the night. Emily went to her room. Mum went to hers. Dad continued to quietly watch TV. The house fell silent. All parties knew some damage had been done but hoped a night's sleep would soften the impact.

Now here is the secret that mum didn't know and needed to know!

Mum thinks Emily is in her room rehearsing how horrible a parent she is. She thinks Emily is visualising her with horns and a pitchfork and planning never to speak to her again!

While this might be true to a certain degree, Emily's thoughts aren't contained there. It is what she thinks about next that is the biggest secret of all.

While in her room Emily is not as tough or self-assured as when she was screaming at her mum. In fact she is crying. She spends most of her time thinking about all the things she knew she did wrong and how right her mother is! She feels guilty, disappointed in herself, and sorry for her actions. Yes, she is sorry for not doing her assignment earlier. She tries to tell herself she doesn't care but she knows she does. She actually cares what her mum thinks!

Because teenagers magnify everything, Emily begins to exaggerate the things her mum said in her mind. By the morning Emily has convinced herself that her mum doesn't love her anymore, that she can never do anything to please her and that her parents would rather she be dead! (A bit extreme, I know, but for many teenagers it isn't far-fetched.) Emily is clinging to and exaggerating any negative message very, very quickly. She is taking everything her mother said to heart and then twisting it some more just to prove how unloved she is.

The next morning mum still thinks Emily is mad because she got busted for not doing her homework, when in fact Emily has moved on to much bigger topics. Emily's mood has intensified when mum hoped it would diminish. Her mother tries to say, 'Good morning' but soon realises her attempts at re-bonding aren't working. Still not understanding the damage done to Emily's fragile self-esteem, she now has bigger problems than the late assignment.

Emily's concept of herself has been damaged in the course of the intense argument the night before. She now thinks less of herself and is heavy inside. Because Emily's view of herself is already fragile she finds it hard to recover quickly and bounce back. Chances are she has also had knocks to her confidence from her peers, so her mother's opinions of her came as a second blow. Emily will need some careful loving to rebuild her confidence.

I know teenagers can do very frustrating and irresponsible things, but I also know that everything you say in the heat of an argument can be taken very seriously and to heart by your teenager. It can cause great damage to your relationship with them. One negative comment you say can remain in their memory for a very long time. One negative word that is not explained thoroughly and said in a controlled and constructive way will be very damaging. Your teenager's confidence is already on shifting sand.

A week in the life of a teenage girl

The journal entry that follows was written by 15-year-old Jasmine who was a part of one of my Youth Excel small group programs. I sat with Jasmine and helped her articulate her thoughts each day as we spent time together. She is a great girl but she was definitely giving her mum a hard time. Reading between the lines I could tell that her mum was at the end of her rope. They were both in the habit of exploding at each other over the big and small issues that were dominating their relationship.

Dear Diary

Monday

Didn't go to school today. I was sick. Did nothing all day but watched movies, ate and slept. Got a big surprise when mum came home earlier than usual and the house was a total pigsty. That immediately started a fight between us. She said she hated me and that she wanted a daughter she could be proud of. She said she wished I hadn't been born because I was destroying the family. That got me saying more hurtful things like I wished she had an abortion. I called her some really bad names and she got so mad. It was funny to see her so mad. After the fight I sat in my room thinking about it and I felt quite bad. I feel really bad when we fight. I heard her on the phone to my dad and I got in trouble from him as well. Had a boring night after that. She took my phone, TV cord and computer away from me. I can't stop thinking about what she said about me. I just feel really bad inside when this happens. She always says she wishes I was someone else. I'm her disappointment. I wish my family was like the happy ones. I can't sleep. It is 2 am.

Tuesday

Went to school today. I was super tired. I almost fell asleep but it was maths so it didn't matter. I hate it when that happens. Had an alright day. It was nice to be away from mum who hates me so much. I don't know why she even calls me her child if she hates me that much. I don't know why she even bothers speaking to me. I feel like crap. I should have never been born. Mum is trying to talk to me like normal again, which is really annoying me. I hate being here. I hate her. No one understands me here. I don't know why I even bother living. I'm going to my friend's house tomorrow afternoon. I can't wait.

Wednesday

I went to Jo's house today. Her mum and her get along so good. She is like so cool. I told her all about mum and my fight and she was really understanding. She would never say she hated Jo. They don't fight that much except for when Jo wants to do stuff she isn't allowed. They wouldn't fight if the house was a mess. I wish I had a mum like that who loved me. Jo's mum always understands me. My mum just yells at me all the time. She doesn't even want to understand what is going on in my life. I'm sick of everyone starting rumours about me at school. Bitching is so stupid and Jo is like my only friend. I don't feel like I fit in too well with my old group. No one likes me, not even my own family. She says I need to say sorry but she should be the one saying sorry to me.

Thursday

I had the biggest fight with Lee today. Here's what happened. Christine (my ex best friend) was saying stupid stuff to me during lunch and he was like, 'I can abuse you all I want. No one is going to do anything about it.' Then I looked at Jo and she said nothing. So I walked off and then she came after me saying sorry. I pushed her away and walked off and I was seriously sad. But we are okay now. When I got home my mum said, 'What's wrong with you?' and that started a massive fight again. This time she said I was ridiculous and she can't stand the sight of me. That's it. I can't stand it anymore. I am in so much trouble again because I told her I hate her. No one understands. I just want everything to go away and be ok again like it used to.

> **Friday**
> *I had a really bad day today because I had a fight with a girl at school who doesn't like me. I hate it when she calls me names so I pushed her. It reminds me of mum when she yells at me. She is such a cow. I can't believe anyone likes her. She always starts rumours about me. The teacher saw and I got into trouble. Mum said she is taking me out to the shops tonight and I can buy some clothes.*
>
> **XX Jasmine (with the help of Michelle)**

Jasmine said she was genuinely affected by the arguments she was having with her mum. As you can see from reading the diary, teenagers not only exaggerate, but allow their exaggerated feelings to affect every area of their life. I often wondered exactly what her mum had said, as opposed to what she heard her mum say. Whatever the case, she was internalising every negative comment and her immaturity made it difficult for her to put herself in her mother's shoes.

How parents can help

You know your daughter has had a bad day when you can feel them coming before you see them. Their vibe literally penetrates the house before they even place a foot in the door. As they finally swing the front door open and slam their school bag on the ground, the tiled floor automatically turns into eggshells and the house pets run for their life! You know you are in for a great afternoon.

At that moment *everything* you say and do is under the microscope. In those moments of super sensitivity, every word you say is magnified, analysed and exaggerated (at least another 100%). They watch your every response and are ready to jump down your throat if you add to their pain. You might feel yourself absorbing your teenager's stress like a dry sponge and before long you are oozing tension!

Many parents genuinely don't know what to do in this type of situation. They feel helpless and they begin to worry. They worry whether their daughter's behaviour is normal. They worry about what happened at school and whether their confidence has been permanently damaged. They worry about them learning how to handle rejection well. They worry about them liking their appearance and believing in their talents. And why do they worry? Simply because they realise that a strong self-esteem is a teenager's number one key to success and happiness in life.

Parents often ask me, 'How can I be a support to her when she is so obviously struggling? I feel terrible seeing her so down on herself and sad. It breaks my heart to see her so unhappy.' Outlined below is an honest list of some of the most important things a parent can do when their teenager is feeling down. You may notice that worrying didn't make the list!

Provide them with consistency

Teenagers need consistency. They need to know that after their world has come to an end you will be the same boring old parent that you were yesterday. They need to know you will treat them the same way even when others have changed the way they treat them. They need to know there are some things you won't say, even in anger.

Of course you are welcome to add in some approval, affirmation, support and encouragement, but remember it needs to be fairly consistent with the day before. There is no need to offer them a barrage of fake compliments. What will support them more than anything is experiencing stability when they feel like their world is out of control.

Respect the way they process pain

It doesn't take rocket science to figure out when a teenager has been emotionally hurt. During these times try to remember that they need time to process their pain before they move on. Try to respect their opinion, their space (they might not be up for a chat!), and their right to be feeling terrible. Don't push too hard for a 'let's fix it' conversation. Avoid nagging, lecturing or demoralising them for being down and most importantly, don't ever dismiss their negative feelings or ignore them. You can show you respect the level of pain they are experiencing by accepting their need to process it the best way they can.

Talk about feelings of inadequacy

Before teenagers embark on a serious conversation with their parents they usually 'test the waters' to see if their choice of conversation will be accepted. If you are privileged enough to pass their test, take the opportunity to talk naturally about feelings of inadequacy with your teenager. It is really easy for girls to think that everyone else has it together except for them. It is good for them to hear that everyone feels inadequate, even adults, and often things turn out okay. It is important that they realise highs and lows are a normal part of life's journey.

Beware of competition at home

Sibling rivalry can be a very vicious source of erosion to teenage self-esteem. Parents should be very aware of factors within the home that will aggravate a teenager's struggling self-esteem. Even passing comments like, 'You have a bad attitude just like your father did' or 'Why don't you try as hard as your brother?' aren't going to help things. Try to treat your teenagers an individuals and be aware of having expectations that don't fit them.

Use the bread roll technique

Most people have heard of the sandwich technique, which is designed to lighten the blow of confrontation — one positive, one negative and then one positive. I prefer to use the bread roll technique with teenagers. This technique is the same as the sandwich technique but involves quadrupling the positives. Try four positives, one negative and then four positives. I don't mean literally listing four positives, but rather being conscious of spending approximately that amount of time proportionately in each area, especially when they are feeling down.

Help them be their best

Everyone feels better about themselves when they are doing something they are good at. Teenagers need to spend a lot of time developing their talents, achieving their goals and simply doing the things they love. It will help them to feel balanced and keep negative feelings in perspective. Whether it is drama, art, music, technology, sport, academics, social groups or clubs, developing a teenager's strengths is critical for developing self-esteem. If your teenager is having a difficult time, make sure you schedule lots of time for them to use their talents and succeed at being themselves.

A thing called 'friendship'

In a flash of an eye, teddy bears and Barbie dolls are replaced with thudding rock music, a no-pink dress policy and a 'GET OUT OF MY ROOM' sign. All of a sudden 'sweet' has turned into 'not-so-sweet'. By the time a teenager is 13, the nasty, competitive and downright bitchy side of girls often lurks on the horizon. Unfortunately, 'friends' can bring out the worst in girls, and be the biggest complication of their lives.

The schoolyard (followed by the internet as a close second) is the most common place for the sweet and innocent to morph into vicious creatures and grow horns. A classroom full of teenage girls usually involves everyone competing to be the best, tearing each other to shreds and then denying every bit of it. It can be a world of bitchy conversation, backstabbing and harsh judgments.

Teenage friendships are commonly an emotionally fuelled roller-coaster ride full of abrupt ups and downs. The ride can be so fast and unpredictable that most adults can hardly keep up with it. In fact, they find the intensity of it difficult to take seriously. One minute she is my 'best friend' and the next, 'I can't stand the sight of her'. One minute, 'Can I please go to the shops with Amy?' and the next, 'Oh she's a cow and we aren't speaking to each other anymore'.

Take for example the diary of 14-year-old Renee presented below. It outlines the friendship dramas she experiences in a normal week of her teenage life. To any adult it is a totally ridiculous whirlwind. To a teenager it is an upsetting but acceptable and relatively normal part of their life's ups and downs. (I feel exhausted just reading it.)

Dear Diary

Monday

It's like Ellie changed overnight. One day we were best friends, the next we were giving each other dirty looks from across the classroom. Why can't this friendship just be simple? She never understands how I feel, or what I have to say. It's always about her. She never bothers to ask me how I feel about the situation, if she's okay — then it's all okay. I don't understand why she has to treat me so badly, I admit I make mistakes, but not to the extent that she has to treat me like I'm worthless. I thought she was different, I thought we had something in common. Maybe tomorrow it will all be fixed, but then again, maybe not. I just don't know what to do anymore.

Tuesday

Today started off perfectly. Everything was amazing. Until we went to Aviation to play volleyball for inter-school sport. For the whole time my best friend Ellie didn't even talk to me. She hung around with this girl she knows and I absolutely dislike. She keeps ditching me and I'm so sick of it. Sometimes I miss my old best friend. She never ditched me and we were each other's best friend. Ellie is my best friend and she says I am hers, but I'm not her only best friend. She also has Megan, Lucy and Brittany. I mean that's ok but she hangs with them more than with me. Last time we had a fight she said, 'You can't just expect to come back into the group if you dump us.'

Wednesday

Today was pretty s***. Ellie has gotten back with her ex-boyfriend, that completely broke my heart. I feel so replaced and she's starting to ditch me all for him. She promised she wouldn't but I know she will! I don't want our friendship ruined by a boy who will hurt her! She's lying to me and I don't even know what I should do. It's like he's all she cares about. At lunchtime when we are together I can tell he's all she cares about. It's like we aren't even close anymore. I can't help feel jealous and I don't know what to do to make it go away. I don't want to be overprotective and want her all to myself, or make her choose. Either way it is going to hurt me or him and she would probably rather it hurt me. So I guess I will have to put up with it.

Thursday

I was talking to my ex-best friend last night and I really miss her. She said she missed me too and we fully got along with each other again. But when we got to school today I tried to hang out with her and stuff but she clinged to this other girl. She told me she was having troubles with her but maybe not!?? I was ready to give her another chance but I guess it won't work out.

Friday

Didn't go to school today. I felt so tired. I had a fight with Ellie on the chat room and stayed up all night worrying about it over and over until it was morning and the sun was coming into my room. I can't handle it when she says stuff behind my back and I get left just because she wants to hang out with someone else. I HATE her and I don't care if I never speak to her again but the problem is going to school with her. It is going to be so bad. She will spread rumours and then no one will like me.

Saturday

Ellie rang me and said sorry and asked me to the movies today. We are back to being best friends. Have to go and get ready … talk to you tomorrow.

It's probably no surprise then to tell you that teenage relationships are not like the relationships that you and I know. They don't abide by any of the same rules. They don't even have many of the same characteristics. They are complex because they can involve friends who are now enemies and enemies who are now friends. They are fickle because they can change in an instant. They are aggressive because they fight for their own rights rather than the rights of each other.

But parents, before you shake your head in disbelief, understand there is a reason for this insanity! The bottom line is that having friends protects teenagers from being labelled a loser or a loner, and getting picked on. Without friends, teenagers are exposed to a life of misery and torture. There is nothing more painful for a teenager than to not have friends. Because of this, they often do anything and put up with anything to avoid being alone.

This is where bullying gets its licence. Teenagers often tolerate a lot of teasing, backstabbing, mood swings and aggression from their friends. Why? The positives greatly outweigh the negatives. The pain of not having friends is far more severe than the pain of having friends who don't treat them well. Teenagers, like adults, choose the option that has the least perceived cost. In other words, having friends can cost them a lot, but not as much as being alone. I like to call this the business end of teenage friendships.

Dealing with the intricacies of this 'business' can sometimes be a touch difficult to say the least. I recently facilitated one of Youth Excel's girls' programs in a local high school. Although I only had to manage a small group of Year 8 girls I more than had my hands full. They were out of control, with defiant behaviour, older boyfriends, binge drinking and — not to my surprise — bullying. They were all having major friendship troubles.

Two of the girls in the group were 'best friends'. Unfortunately, they were best friends who loved to hate each other! In an attempt to solve their problems, they had created a set of strict guidelines. Their guidelines restricted each other's behaviour in order to minimise the constant arguments. They weren't allowed to talk to anyone else, they weren't allowed to invite anyone else into their group and they weren't allowed to make plans without telling each other. They were suffocating each other with their jealousy, and fuelling each other's insecurities.

Neither of the girls were happy, but neither of them wanted to move on. In their minds the benefits of being in the friendship outweighed the consequences of being out of it. Each time they 'broke up' they made it so intensely painful for each other that they simply had to get 'back together'. When they got 'back together' they had the best of times, until things turned bad. It was a vicious cycle.

The things these two girls did to each other when they 'broke up' was, from my perspective, extreme and relentless. My ears burned from hearing stories of name calling, ganging up on each other, stealing from each other, starting rumours, making anonymous abusive phone calls and so on. It was a horrible sight.

Most teenage friendships experience this cycle to some degree. The repetition of being together and being apart, of getting along and not getting along, is one that often drives parents crazy. This is especially true of love/hate friendships. It is how teenagers treat each other when things aren't going well and 'hate' is in full swing that does the most damage.

But your teenage daughter's behaviour hides an important secret. It is a secret that most girls who are in conflict hold onto tightly.

Both girls, quite separately but quite purposefully, hide the worst of each other's behaviour from the adults in their lives. They choose to leave out all the extremely hurtful details and keep information to the bare minimum. It wasn't that their parents and the school counsellor didn't know that they were constantly fighting, but they had no idea of what was really going on. Everyone thought it was just girl dramas, when things were far worse.

Your teenager will rarely tell you exactly how horrible their friends are to them. If you are lucky they might tell you about 50% of what their enemies do to them! Teenagers withhold this information from their parents, sometimes out of embarrassment, or at other times because they don't want you involved. The bottom line is that they know you won't approve. They want you to like their friends so that next time they are asked out they are allowed to go!

The other thing that they probably won't tell you is their own contribution to the problem. They don't tell you exactly what they did or said. They won't want you looking at any records of their messages, emails, or texts. They would prefer you to believe they are totally innocent and the victim, which is almost never the case.

When you ask them, 'What's wrong? Why hasn't Shannon rung?' and they say, 'Nothing much. I'm not talking to her anymore', you will know exactly what that means. It means they are treating or being treated in a way that you wouldn't approve of. It is only late at night, when they are really feeling vulnerable that the truth (and probably only half of it) comes out and they tell you how hurt they really are.

In this way the turbulence of teenage friendships is often hidden from parents who seldom really see or understand just how common a part of their teenager's daily lives bullying is. What your teenager wants you to understand more than anything is that they need the friendship more than life itself. They also want you to know that despite the drama associated with it, they can't live without having a group they belong to. Anything that could possibly jeopardise their friendship will remain a secret.

The following two stories show how much teenagers try to hide the worst of their friendship dramas from their parents. I hope parents realise through reading these passages that their daughters sometimes try to protect you from their pain just as much as you try to protect them. I also hope you understand that just because your daughter is talking about her friendship dramas doesn't mean she is telling you everything. Chances are she is leaving the worse bits out.

She's my best friend forever

I used to have a friendship group then they started trying to teach me how to eat. The group decided to put me on a diet. They said if I didn't lose weight I wouldn't be allowed to be in the group anymore. And they were monitoring me and I hated it so much. No one understood that I have a medical condition and I can't lose weight. No one believed me. I'm not in the group now and I don't have many friends. I lost my confidence around people because of everything that happened. I don't care about having friends any more. When I went swimming at school they would all tease me and say I was fat and that I shouldn't be swimming and make me go away. They would call me a whale and fat ass and stuff like that. I never told my parents what happened at swimming and I never told them about the diet they put me on. They think I just didn't want to go. They would get really mad if I told them and my dad might go to the school and that would be really embarrassing and make things worse. Everyone in my family is fat. It's not that easy to just lose weight. I think some girls are just born skinny and I'm born fat. No one likes fat people but I don't care.

Amy, age 13

My parents are really REALLY strict and they won't let me have a boyfriend or let him sleep over like Jenna's parents do. They are kind of racist but racist towards people who don't have the same standards as them. They want to choose my friends, which is none of their business. They should love everyone and give them a chance to get to know them. I don't tell them what Jenna does and I tried to make out that she is good so they let me go out with her. When Jenna teases me about not being allowed to do anything it really hurts. Sometimes she posts it on Facebook and rings me when she is at a party with my boyfriend and says she is hooking up with him. I really trust him so I know he won't do anything with her. She tells everyone that my parents are Nazis, which sort of hurts but I hate them too sometimes.

Krystal, age 15

Bullying in your home

Cyber-bullying is a term I am sure you have heard of. It describes all forms of bullying that can happen over the internet. Cyber-bullying is a very common form of bullying among teenagers, and one that comes directly into your home and impacts on your family time. It can change the mood of a teenager in seconds. It can interrupt anytime, even when trying to finish up homework for the week or having a meal together.

The most dangerous part of cyber-bullying is that it can take place anytime, whenever another teenager has the desire to be horrid, take out their emotions on someone else or relieve their sense of boredom. It isn't uncommon for teenagers to get together on Saturday night with the sole purpose of bullying others over the internet or via text messages on a mobile phone. It gives them a high — all in the comfort of their own home.

Cyber-bullying has the potential to impact on a teenager, as much as technology does. As long as a teenager is connected to a computer or a mobile phone, they can be bullied. Teenagers tend to hide this form of bullying from parents because it can be so graphic! There is something infuriating about seeing derogatory comments about your daughter written in black and white. What is also painful is that those comments can be read over and over again and are never erased.

As a parent, the first thing you want to do is protect your teenagers from any unnecessary forms of bullying. Eliminating bullying all together is unrealistic but the more it can be minimised the better. Because communicating over the internet is a totally different form of communication, it needs a unique set of rules. It can't be compared to face-to-face communication in any way.

SUPERVISION AND MORE SUPERVISION!

The internet — and technology in general — is a tremendous asset, with so many benefits to everyone. It has become a part of our everyday life and I am sure none of us could live without it. However, when it comes to teenagers, the internet and their mobile phone do need to be managed very carefully.

I know you have probably heard this before from other sources but I need to say it also — computers and bedrooms are a recipe for disaster. Computers should only be used in socially active family areas where monitoring is easy for parents. This is even the case if your teenager is swearing black and blue they are doing their English assignment! If adults are not home I would suggest computers not be used at this time as this is when most bullying occurs.

Responding to bullying

There are so many things that can go wrong when a teenager uses the internet alone. First, they are far more likely to react emotionally and in an uncalculated fashion against bullying. Innocent conversations can rapidly spiral downhill. Teenagers can quickly get into conversations and be exposed to things they simply don't know how to handle. The key word here is 'quickly'. They can receive a message in an instant and they have very little control over what messages they receive until they read it. Once they receive it, their response can start a chain reaction they are unprepared for. Even simple messages like, 'Hey Slag. What's happening?' can escalate into a full public war within minutes if not handled well.

The key to avoidance is simple — don't respond. That means using self-control, which many teenagers don't have. Blocking potential bullies, not responding to troublesome texts or messages, is the best way to combat cyber-bullying. If a bully fails to get a response they are likely to stop. If things continue, you have a solid record of the bullying that can be taken to the police or school if necessary.

Sexual activity

Teenagers, even teenage girls, are quite commonly exposed to many forms of pornography on the internet. Nude or semi-nude photos of young people are quite commonly posted on the net or sent to mobile phones. I recently came across a group of young men who were photographing their penises and sending them to their girlfriends, encouraging them to photograph their breasts and send them back. Sexual activity on the internet is very common. It is amazing how pressured young people feel to be involved in such activities and how quickly they can get caught up in it.

Nothing is private

Teenagers need to continually remember that nothing posted on the net is private. Even if their friends say they won't show or tell anyone, it is so easy for a message or post to leak or be found. Once a teenager has sent an email, posted something on Facebook or sent a message via a chat room you can't assume the emails or messages will remain private. It means if a teenager badmouths a girl in her grade, that girl will see it. Teenagers need to know that they should not write anything they aren't prepared to become front-line news. Once something is said in anger it can't be taken back. Once something private is in writing it can be posted anywhere.

Talk to them

Talk to your teenage daughter about her internet use constantly. If there is an open dialogue between you it is more likely that her concerns will eventually be discussed. Teenagers need to be aware of predators and what to do if they come across them, but they also need to know what to do if their friends introduce them to strangers, pornography, drug deals or graphic language over the net. They need to know that you are educated and that they can ask for help anytime they are in over their heads. Becoming their friend on their Facebook page is a simple start.

Set time limits

Time limits provide another level of safety for internet communication. Teenagers need space from the computer and time out from their social world. I would suggest parents decide a time limit based on balance. The time they spend on the computer should be no more than they spend on their homework or other interests and hobbies. This allows time for the intensity of teenage conversation to die down.

Get an internet filter

There are a host of internet filters that parents can purchase for their home computer. There are programs that will block, alert and track internet use. I would highly recommend that any computer a teenager or child uses is protected by such programs. Your local computer store will be able to direct you to the best on the market.

When friendship dramas become serious bullying

Each teenager has a highly individual journey when it comes to friendships. Some seem to coast through high school years with a relatively stable group of friends. Others experience a far more challenging road. It is very common for teenagers to have an inner circle of friends who they trust, and a group who they love to hate. Most teenagers experience the complexity of relating to friends and enemies (or potential enemies) each day.

There is a fine line between friendship dramas and bullying. It is often very hard for adults to distinguish the difference. This is because the principles that run a teenager's normal social world are usually the same ones they experience when they are being bullied. They are just more intense. It is also because teenage girl bullying is often a two-way street, so it is hard to find who is the bully and who is the person being bullied, although there is often a clear winner.

To help parents wade through the onslaught of friendship challenges, I suggest they think of bullying on a scale of 1 to 10. The lower levels of bullying are, although not right, very common in a teenager's world. You would have to annihilate every teenager alive in order to eradicate this level of bullying! Low-level bullying might involve occasional name-calling or dirty looks that pass quickly. Here are some really common examples of low-level bullying:

Tina is obviously moody with her best friend. She is rolling her eyes when she speaks and refusing to sit with her at lunch. When pressed on the phone later that night Tina says, 'I am upset because your mother gave birth to such a beautiful girl. I am jealous that you are so pretty. I think Jordan likes you not me!' The next day the mood has passed and she finds out that Jordan does like her after all.

Georgina is chatting on Messenger to her girlfriends after school. She gets a message from another girl which says 'I thought you were my friend but all you are is a b***'. Georgina replies with a few more choice words and things go back and forth till the wee hours of the morning. They are both nervous about school in the morning but instead of continuing the argument Georgina decides to apologise and the two of them spend the day together.

Elizabeth, who has always been Miss Popular, has been experiencing some 'not so nice' comments ever since winning a 'Student with the most potential of succeeding at Uni' award. She felt really good about herself for receiving the award and despite the girls' comments has continued to study and get good grades. Over time the girls' comments have become fewer.

Bullying becomes more damaging when it is constant. Bullying is always very concerning when a teenager feels helpless against it and is limited in their options to handle it. It is always a big concern when a teenager's confidence is shattered because of it and they lose their ability to think creatively to get on top of the problem.

Bullying can take all sorts of forms, including teenagers isolating, threatening, physically fighting or blackmailing each other. Bullies can enjoy humiliating, demoralising and destroying another girl's reputation. Teenage girls are masters at using the 'round up' strategy and seem to enjoy the challenge of getting everyone involved. And this is made so easy thanks to the internet. They can also be masters at making it look like they didn't do anything wrong and can often very cleverly hide their nastiness from teachers and parents.

And don't be fooled into thinking aggression is for boys! Teenager girls have a double whammy. They can be both physically and emotionally aggressive. They can enjoy punching a girl's 'lights out', catching it on camera and then bragging to the world about it over the internet. The aggression that is coming from girls seems to be growing and is a culture new to many parents. In today's schools girls are cool if they are tough. They aspire to be physically strong and able to win a fist fight.

It can be ugly and shocking to see how unimaginably merciless girls can be. I often find myself thinking 'Surely they can't have done that to her' when I realise that in fact they did. Because teenagers are unlikely to tell their parents the extent of the bullying they are experiencing, parents should be vigilant in watching for warning signs. Some of them include:

- sudden change in personality style — more passive and sad
- sudden change in friendship circle
- sudden loss of confidence
- difficultly answering simple questions about friends
- consistently withdrawn
- not wanting to go to school
- feeling generally 'sick', increased headaches, general pains, stomach upsets that may be anxiety based.

Talking with your daughter about bullying

The following letter is a teenager's attempt to tell her mum that she is not coping with the bullying she is experiencing at school. I often hear teenagers describing a friendship situation they feel overwhelmed with. They go to great lengths to look and sound overwhelmed, only to have the adults in their lives roll their eyes as if to say, 'Here we go again! Can't you just get over it!' Two challenges face parents — first, when to take things seriously, and second, what to do about it.

> To Mum,
> This is what is happening at school. All my friends are fighting. I might be acting like it is all right but it's not. Carolyn, Liz, Dani and Rhonda are fighting and my self-esteem is very low! It is so hard to be friends with people who like the person who hates you. It was two weeks ago they started on me. Every time you be yourself they slap you — if you say

> *something they don't like they slap you. When I come home and said I wanted to change groups, you said 'Just tell them to stop'. You don't understand. I know you like my group and you want me to have friends but I can't keep going like this. I feel humiliated so bad and I cry all the time and you don't even know. School is a nightmare and you just say it's normal. All you know is what you did at your age. Well mum, that was 27 years ago. Now its 2010 and bitches and friendships have changed. I'm not you! I want to change groups but there is nowhere to go.*
>
> **by Sugar, aged 16**

There is always a huge gap between the adult and teenage world, but none more so than in the way friends relate to each other. Because of this, most of the advice that parents give teenagers is simply not going to work in their world.

The teenage world is so dramatically different to the world of an adult and therefore requires different skills to survive. It is understandable that you feel the need to prepare your teenager for the adult world, but don't forget how important it is to prepare them for the world that they are living in now. If your teenager is being bullied, help your teenager cope with their world. If you feel like you can't help them for whatever reason, seek professional help and find someone who can.

What is most important is that you show your teenager that you care. What will demonstrate this more than anything else is your ability to provide relevant, sensible advice that relates to their situation. You have to equip yourself to have a productive and helpful discussion with them about bullying. To assist you, here some pointers I give teenagers who are struggling with bullying.

'You can't beat a bully by being a bully'

Chances are your teenager will get bullied on a small scale fairly regularly. They are more likely to continue to be bullied if they react to that bullying. Crying, pouting, and fighting back are all signs that the bully has power over them and that their methods are working. It has the bully coming back for more every time. Don't teach your teenager to defend themselves by calling the bully a worse name or threatening to bash them up. There is a great chance that the girl who has started the fight is stronger than them and has the ability to beat them hands down. Never teach them to beat a bully by being a bully. Instead, think of bullying like squeezing a tomato sauce bottle. If there isn't any sauce left, you might shake it for a while but then get bored with it and give up. Bullying is the same. If there is no reaction, bullies eventually lose interest.

'You can't just walk away'

Teenagers are often told that the only alternative to fighting a bully is to simply walk away. The advice 'walk away' in real-life, practical terms does not always work. If teenagers feel that all they can do is 'walk away', they feel defeated. What we don't want is your daughter walking away, totally crushed, ready to replay in her mind later that night, in the quiet dark of her bedroom, every word the bully has said to her. In the same way you don't beat a bully by being a bully, you don't beat a bully by cowering and slinking away. There is more to the solution than that!

'You have to know you are okay'

Teenagers truly beat a bully, and potentially reduce further bullying, when they walk away from a bully with their head held high, knowing they are still okay. There is a big difference between walking away defeated and walking away knowing that you are okay, that you have options and that you can be proactive about turning things around. This can actually happen!

'You may have to pretend'

Chances are that no teenager will feel 'okay' after being called a 'retard' in front of the whole Year level. I recommend a little acting at this point. Smart teenagers pretend they are still okay by holding their heads high and shrugging off the comments. Teenagers need to give the impression that the bully doesn't hold as much power as they think they do. If your teenager comes home from school with a huge emotional reaction there is a high possibility they have pretended to be okay at school all day and you are now receiving the reaction they felt like showing at school.

'You need to know what to say back'

Teenagers feel equipped when they have good comeback lines. However, they should remember that the strong don't need to defend themselves. Comeback lines are attacking and create more bullying. If a teenager acts bored or uninterested in the bully it is the best comeback line they can use. Alternatively, here are some responses that maybe useful — 'If you say so', 'I can't argue with that', 'That's a pretty strong statement', 'I have nothing to say', 'That's a pretty good point', 'I'll think about it', 'I agree' or 'I disagree and that's okay'. Agreeing with a bully usually dissolves things quickly.

'You can't cope alone'

Communicating with another person is a great way to process the negativity of bullying. Communicating can help teenagers decide what is true and right, what is their fault and what is not, what they feel and why, and what they can do tomorrow. This can be a challenge however, given that bullying is a subject most young people are hesitant and embarrassed to talk about on a deep level. Talking about bullying makes them feel inadequate. It requires that they verbalise their insecurities and anxieties. This is not something that is easy for teenagers, and parents should really appreciate their teenagers when they do open up on this level.

'You must have hidden support'

Confident teenagers have hidden support. They might not admit to it but they have adult back-up. They have places to turn when things go wrong. It is important that every teenager has a safe adult who can talk through their friendship challenges. If you aren't able to talk openly with your teenager, consider helping them build a relationship with their favourite aunty, grandmother, school guidance officer, sports coach, chaplain or youth group leader.

'You can rely on me to be nobody'

I recently heard one mum tell her daughter this: 'When your friends tell you a secret and make you swear to tell 'nobody' I want you to always remember that I can be 'nobody'. This way you can keep your promise to your friends and you don't have to carry the secret alone.' This is a great way to approach communication about bullying. It has to be a confidential conversation that they feel very safe having.

'You need to understand what I can't do'

Your teenager has to understand that you can't fight their battles for them. Heading up to the principal's office with a hot head isn't really going to help your teenager's cause. Realise that the answer to your teenager's friendship problems lies within them rather than within you. As much as you would like to, you can't fix your teenager's problems for them. In most cases, an overinvolved parent can make things much worse. Teenagers are the only ones who can truly turn the situation around and it usually has to come from the inside out.

'You need to understand what I can do'

Your teenager needs to know that you want to contribute something valuable to their situation. If necessary, buy them resources about teenage bullying and let them know you can provide them with more professional help if they need it. Take their feelings seriously and treat them the way you would like to be treated.

'You need to learn to laugh at yourself'

Encourage your teenager to try to make light of a bully's taunts instead of reacting. Unfortunately, teenagers who take themselves too seriously are often the victim of bullying. Try to help your teenager be lighthearted about their mistakes and failures, so they will realise that it will keep others from picking on them. Help them realise that bullies often ride in on others' insecurities and enjoy magnifying their victims' faults because they know it will give them the greatest reaction. Almost every teenager gets bullied at some point. It is how they deal with it that either magnifies or minimises it.

'You need to feel proud of yourself'

It is important that every teenager has something to be proud of. Whether it be dance, music, their new hairstyle or the latest dress they bought, self-pride is important as it affects the way they carry themselves. Bullies are likely to pick on the teenager who is standing with the least confidence. Help your teenager stand taller by doing everything you can to develop their talents and take care of their appearance.

'You need to realise your appearance matters'

Cool clothes do matter. It is almost impossible for a teenager to be confident if they don't feel comfortable with their appearance. Clothes aren't a waste of money. They are an investment in your teenager's feeling of self-worth. That doesn't mean that they need to shop every weekend, but it is important that parents realise how the teenage pecking order operates. Use it to your teenager's advantage. If a new outfit makes that much difference in a teenager's lowest moments, then embrace it.

'You need to consider forgiveness'

Teenagers have the ability to dramatically change their opinion and behaviour from one day to the next. Often the memory of yesterday's bullying doesn't line up with the friends' behaviour today. Teenagers can get stuck holding grudges based on yesterday's behaviours. This can really limit their ability to interact freely today. Encourage your teenager to treat every day as new, forgiving faults as much as possible. Giving friends a second chance is something that most teenagers need to do. Forgiveness doesn't mean that other people are allowed to continue to treat you wrongly. Forgiveness says 'I can move on from the pain of yesterday and approach you with an open mind today'. If bullying is consistent, encourage teenagers to forgive and then make the choices they need to in order to protect themselves.

'You need to look out for others'

There is an old saying that suggests that whatever you give to others, it will be given back to you. In other words, however you treat others will determine how others will treat you. If you always do your best to be kind and try to get along with everyone, you will have too many people supporting you for a bully to gain too much ground. Encourage your teenager to eliminate strong words like 'whore' or 'slag' from their vocabulary. Talk to them about avoiding conversations that are downright nasty. If she can be the person who sticks up for others who are being taken advantage of, chances are that others will stick up for her. Being consistently nice is the best way to combat a bully in the long term.

Chapter 5

Why don't you trust me?

I want you to protect me

❖

For goodness sake, don't trust them!

Many years ago I received a phone call at 2 am from a teenager who told me she had been assaulted. She was hysterical and it sounded like her very life hung in the balance. I jumped out of bed, with images of bloodshed overtaking my mind. I alerted the police and then drove like a lunatic to the scene. I, Miss Super Youth Worker, was ready to save the day! On my arrival I found out that I had been totally conned. She hadn't been assaulted at all. In fact, she had actually assaulted a policewoman!

It is behaviour like this that has taught me to be cautious about trusting a teenager. Sure, I'd trust them to put out the garbage or cross the road safely — I *might* even trust them to do their homework. But I couldn't give them the same trust I would give a mature adult. There are simply too many risks associated with giving teenagers your complete trust too quickly.

Although I am not denying that on the odd occasion you may find a heroic teenager who defies all odds and triumphs over peer pressure, such cases are the exception. Even then it is unlikely that teenagers will be able to continue to make good choices under consistent pressure. Teenagers are not mini-adults. They are teenagers and the difference between the two is far greater than most adults realise.

Teenagers have a thought process that is unique to their own world. They don't think like an adult, even if they look like one! Being able to use 'grown-up' words and concepts doesn't automatically equate to adult thinking. A teenager's brain function is also still developing. Because of this they have the potential to make life-changing decisions without calculating risk or using foresight. This means that teenagers don't have to be bad kids to get into serious trouble.

For some reason, teenagers honestly believe that their parents should, by inherent right, trust them because they have turned 13. I see many parents trusting their teenagers because they feel pressured to do so, not because it makes good parenting sense. Trust is a concept that is argued about relentlessly in most teenage homes. It seems to come up in every second conversation, usually after last week's binge drinking and before the part about wanting to go out on the weekend. Teenagers dare their parents to trust them, even when their behaviour is totally untrustworthy.

Most parents do realise that it takes more than the ability to blow out 13 candles to handle life, but they also hope to be proven wrong. They hope their daughter will be the one to set a new benchmark in trustworthiness. They offer their trust only to find that they should have listened to their better judgment in the first place.

What every parent needs is a bucketload of confidence that empowers them to say 'no', whenever they feel the need to. Parents need to realise that it's okay for them to say 'no' at any time, for any logical reason, including not feeling comfortable. You are the parent and you have a great responsibility — the responsibility to protect your child.

I regularly hear teenagers complain that their parents don't trust them and that they are not allowed to do anything they want to. This comforts me far more than it concerns me. Parents who say 'no' simply care enough about their child to protect them. After all, it's easier to turn a blind eye and hope that everything is going to be okay. It takes a lot more effort, in the short term, to know where your teenager is and what they are doing.

Parents are usually under a lot of pressure to trust their teenager. However, I would like to suggest that it's not your job to trust them. It is your job to protect them. Of course, that's not to say your teenager will immediately understand the link between trust and protection. I frequently talk with teenagers who are frustrated by their parents' need to 'control' their lives. I usually look them straight in the eye and say, 'I know you will understand this because I know you know what teenagers have the potential to get up to. It's not your parent's job to trust you. They don't *have* to trust you right now. It's their job to *protect* you.'

The best advice I could ever give a parent is — expect your teenager to act like a teenager and expect to have to be their parent. Trust is not something that teenagers should have the power to negotiate. You decide how much trust your daughter is given. Do yourself a favour as a parent and take the issue of trust off the table as a bargaining tool. Don't feel pressured to offer more of your trust as a reward for good behaviour. Parents should weigh each decision carefully against the potential risks and the current social pressure their teenager is facing. The following true story illustrates the importance of not trusting your teenager against your better judgment.

Sarah's story

Earlier this year I sat in McDonalds with 15-year-old Sarah. She was a beautiful girl who looked like she was about to turn 18. She was very bright and articulate, with both academic and sporting successes. She looked like a model student who had it all together, and was well-mannered in front of me. But at home, it was a different story.

Sarah's mum had contacted me earlier in the week to explain that they were experiencing intense arguments with Sarah at home. She told me how exasperated her husband was and how great an impact the tension was having on their marriage and their other children. Sarah's group of friends seemed to be allowed to do things that Sarah's family were very uncomfortable with. Drinking, smoking and 'sleeping around' seemed to be normal and accepted by their families. Things came to a head when her father found a fake ID and a packet of cigarettes in Sarah's room.

As I spoke to her, Sarah's complaints were typical of most teenagers. She wanted more freedom and fewer rules. She wanted to make her own decisions. She wanted to be trusted to handle her own life. She wanted to advance to GO and collect $200, right now, even though it wasn't her turn. According to Sarah, her life was confined to nothing more than schoolwork and home chores. There were no parties, no big-ticket spending, no staying out late, or having boyfriends older than her.

As I sat there, I could feel the barrage of relentless pressure from across the table — and I wasn't even her mother! She had carefully crafted arguments as to why she should be allowed to make her own decisions. She had identified the personal weaknesses of her parents, just to prove that they weren't perfect either. She was absolutely guaranteeing that if her mum trusted her, she would do the right thing.

Sarah was understandably frustrated with the situation and I was getting frustrated just listening to her. She felt like her family was controlling her every move. Yet, as I listened, I had to somewhat agree. She was right. Her parents were attempting to control her behaviour and to not do so could have resulted in grave consequences. To let that girl out of her parents' sight could have been disastrous.

Her parents' genuine love demanded that they say 'no' even though it wasn't popular. Love challenged them to stand strong in the face of the protesting, arguing and rebelling in order to keep Sarah safe. Her parents needed to be prepared to fight for her future, apply tough boundaries and a lot of support.

A few months passed. Sarah had been grounded and things had begun to settle down until Bonnie, one of Sarah's 'better' friends, invited Sarah over for a sleep-over. The only problem was that Bonnie's parents weren't going to be home. Sarah had been relentlessly asking her mum if she could sleep over at Bonnie's during every waking moment of the entire week. The final conversation went something like this:

'Please, please let me go mum. I am only going to be sleeping over at Bonnie's house. You've let me go to Bonnie's before! Why won't you let me go now?'

'I have already told you Sarah,' her mum replied. 'I am not comfortable with her parents not being home. I wouldn't usually let you be at home alone.'

'What's the big deal with that?' Sarah exclaims. 'I am old enough to stay home! Don't you trust me? Tiffany's mum trusts her. She leaves her home alone all the time. You think I am so irresponsible. Haven't you noticed I am changing? If you trusted me you would let me go! I can't believe that I am the only one who is not allowed to stay home alone!'

'I can't keep going on about this Sarah. I don't want to talk about it anymore.'

'But mum if you just let me go I'll stop going on!'

Sarah's persistence began wearing her mother down.

'I will call you on my mobile like every hour if you want. It's not like anything bad is going to happen. *All* we will be doing is watching DVDs. She will be really disappointed if I don't go. I am her only friend and she is counting on me. She is going through a really hard time and needs me. You have to let me go.'

There is a moment of silence. Sarah's mum's head is spinning. She feels enormous pressure. And then, in a momentary lapse of judgment, she relents. 'If I let you go you have to promise me you are going to behave yourself this time. No alcohol. No movies I wouldn't approve of. You know I am trusting you.'

With a sudden change of attitude and a twinkle in her eye, sweet Sarah returns. 'I promise mum. Thank you so much. I won't disappoint you again. You are the best!'

Everyone is happy. The pressure is over!

But six weeks later the truth about Sarah and Bonnie's slumber party comes crashing into their lives. Sarah presents her parents with the results of a positive pregnancy test. There is no doubt it stems from the night she stayed at Bonnie's house 'watching movies'. Sarah's family now have a lot more pressure to handle than saying 'no' to a movie night. It isn't their fault Sarah is pregnant. Her parents were genuinely doing their best. Regardless, it has changed the course of all of their lives.

When I heard about Sarah's predicament I couldn't help thinking back to that conversation we had at McDonalds and the secret she so quickly told me. I had actually asked Sarah whether her mum had reason to not trust her. She replied: 'Absolutely, but don't go and tell mum that will you?!' I also asked her if she would trust herself. She automatically said, 'No way. Of course I wouldn't be that stupid to trust me!' She looked at me like I had gone mad. She knew she was untrustworthy! She knew that she needed saving from herself, even before she asked her mother about spending the night at Bonnie's.

Avoid being manipulated

Parents need to wise up to the strategies teenagers use to manipulate them into saying 'yes' when they should be saying 'no'. Once you know these strategies they are the most predictable of all teenage behaviours and they are actually their biggest secrets. Parents, please have your eyes open to these strategies. Keep them firmly in your mind and, if necessary, come back to these strategies when you are feeling so inundated with pressure that you are about to make a decision you may later regret.

Manipulation Strategy 1: Beginning the conversation with, 'Why don't you trust me?'

Whenever your daughter uses the word 'trust' it should ring warning bells in your ears. When a conversation begins with

'Why don't you trust me?' you are best assuming that something is up. Keeping the conversation focused on trust is the very first thing that many teenagers do when they want their own way. Teenagers want to make their parents feel obligated to trust them. I don't know how many times I have seen, 'Why don't you trust me?' sandwiched between two lies — one about where they will be going and then next about what they will be doing.

Manipulation Strategy 2: Presenting an overly detailed story

Teenagers are experts at making up elaborate stories in order to divert attention away from what they are really up to. They have an ability to present a detailed, convincing story fit for an Academy Award. You need to listen very carefully to any complex explanation and follow its logic in the light of what you already know about your daughter, her friends, and her recent activities. Also remember that if the story doesn't add up, then it probably isn't true, and if you detect one small lie the chances are there are bigger ones also involved.

Manipulation Strategy 3: Hiding communication with friends

Before mobile phones, email, and social networking websites, there was usually one main phone at home in the middle of the lounge room. Parents could hear every conversation their teenager had with their friends. These days, teenage communication is much more private. The downside to modern technology is it is much easier for teenagers to hide behaviour and organise themselves without their parents even knowing. Parents need to be more diligent to observe when their daughter might be secretively communicating with her friends.

Manipulation Strategy 4: Making your life miserable

Teenagers often create the 'parent pressure cooker' scenario on purpose. They gang up on parents deliberately, knowing exactly what they are doing. When a teenager wants her own way, especially if she has a lot riding on it, she will pull out all stops to see it happen. Teenagers know that every human being has a limit and at some point you are likely to crack. They also know your weaknesses and how to use those to their advantage. Your role as a parent is to first accept that you will feel pressured, then try to avoid making decisions out of this pressure.

Setting rules

Teenagers make me laugh when they are overtaken by moments of honesty. I don't know why they do it, but they seem to need to spill the beans every now and then. I asked Stephanie, a young girl I was mentoring, to write an open letter to parents on the topic of whether teenagers need rules. What she had to say was priceless!

> *Dear Parents*
>
> *Michelle asked me to write a letter to you about whether I think you can trust your teenager or not. Let me introduce myself. I am a normal 14-year-old girl who goes to a local*

Why don't you trust me?

state high school. I don't get into trouble at school that much, except for detentions for wearing makeup. I am not the naughtiest kid in the school. I am about average.

I think three out of four kids lie to their parents. You would be surprised how many kids lie. I rarely meet a teenager who doesn't lie. We even lie to our friends. I lie to my parents all the time about what I do. I smoke and they don't even know. I drink sometimes too and they would die if they found about it so I am not going to tell them.

You can't trust your teenager. Teenagers will lie to your face if they think they might get into trouble. You may think your child is a sweet little angel but they are mostly not. Teenagers are all about being the coolest, most popular girl and boy in the school. Kids are secretly doing stuff you don't want to know about. They say they are going to be at a friend's house, but instead they go to a party with alcohol and drugs and much older boys who will take advantage of the underage girls without thinking twice. That is what happens when girls drink.

This is my recent lying story …

Mum thought I was having a normal sleep-over, and I was until we jumped on a chat room and got an instant message from a boy in Year 11 at our school. He invited us over to his house because he was with a friend and they were bored. We waited until our parents were asleep, which was about 11.30 pm. We stuffed the sleeping bags and quietly crept out of the back door. We called a taxi at the bottom of the street. When the taxi came we jumped in the cab.

When we got to his house his parents were on holidays. We jumped into bed (head to tail). Nothing bad happened. We drank some alcohol and stayed up until 4 am. Then we thought we better get home before we got busted. We had no money so we tried to walk home. We walked for two hours to the train station. We got on the train and then walked to my house.

When we got to my house my sister was on the front lawn looking for us. She said, 'Mum is so angry.' Mum said, 'You are moving schools.' Then she turned to my friend and said, 'You are never coming over again.' Mum sent me to my room but I could still hear everything. We told mum we went to Shannon's, who is another one of our friends. If she knew we went to a boy's house she would kill me even more. She believed that I went to Shannon's, thank God!

I was grounded for 3 months. Mum still doesn't like my friend and she never knows what really happened ... until she reads this book. Don't kill me mum. I have been good ever since then.

I hope you learnt something about teenagers from my story. You can't trust them and if you do you are crazy because the ones whose parents believe them do the worst stuff. They do stupid stuff and that is just what teenagers do. All my friends do and they joke about what they get away with to look cool.

Love from Stephanie

Keeping things on track

Rules help provide a safety net of protection for teenagers. However, rules are only valid as long as they keep serving their protective purpose. Keeping rules for the sake of keeping them has no worth. Parents should assess the effectiveness of their rules in context with how their young person is developing. From time to time rules will need to be changed in order to serve their purpose. I find that parents commonly worry about how and when to change rules without causing civil war! It is a concern well-warranted as I have noticed many families struggle through this transition. Here are some real-life examples from families who have needed to change the rules.

Heidi was fighting with her best friend at school. She was getting emotionally distraught before going to bed at night and this was affecting her sleep patterns. Due to the extra stress she was feeling, she was allowed to 'unwind' by playing on the computer until late at night. This was something she wasn't previously allowed to do. There were also a few times when she was so upset that she was allowed to skip school for a day or two. Again, this was not part of the family's regular rules. Heidi is now refusing to go to school and wanting to stay up late every night playing computer games. Her parents realised that they need to reintroduce their regular rules in order to protect Heidi.

Jessie is given more freedom because she has turned 16. She is allowed to go to the movies unsupervised and stay out until 10 pm on the weekends. Soon after giving Jessie this new freedom, her parents found out that some of her close friends had been caught shoplifting when they should have been at the movies. Jessie's parents have decided to keep a closer track on where Jessie is and what she is doing. She is not allowed to go to the movies with the friends who were caught shoplifting.

Both these situations demand that parents step in and redirect their teenager's behaviour. In both cases, parents are likely to have a battle on their hands while their teenager adjusts to the new rules. Parents might be tempted to put off making the changes in light of the battle they know they will face. Yet the strongest message of love you can send your teenager is when you are prepared to go out of your way to protect them. As exhausting as it may be, it tells volumes to your teenager about your commitment to them — it actually makes them feel safe. Here are some steps that may help parents adjust the rules in their household.

Step 1: Be honest

A positive change in the short term doesn't always mean a positive in the long term. Your teenager may initially appear less stressed, happier and more compliant with a temporary rule relaxation. It can be a necessary mood breaker for the whole family. However, over a longer period of time parents may notice that teenagers are developing habits that may clearly damage their future. Teenagers need to know the honest reason for your concerns before you change the rules.

Step 2: Create the right mindset

Teenagers firstly need to understand that rules are never set in concrete. Parents have the privilege of assessing the family rules and changing them at any time, as they deem necessary. Parents should feel free to assess each situation and make decisions based on what is best for everyone at that time.

Step 3: Think through consequences ahead of time

Before you change a rule you should know what you will do if your teenager refuses to comply. Parents should have a clear set of consequences in place in case they need to use them. It is also worth having back-up consequences planned if the initial consequences have no effect. You may not need to communicate these consequences to your teenager straight away. However, knowing your options will strengthen your confidence and ability to follow through.

Step 4: Have realistic expectations

Mental preparation arms parents with the stamina to face their teenager's reaction. You should try to anticipate how your teenager will react by thinking about the issue from their side. No one likes a loss of freedom, especially teenagers. You should expect them to feel strong emotions. Try to provide lots of positive places where they can release their emotional energy in a healthy way.

Step 5: Create positive experiences

Plan to reinforce your love for your daughter. Introduce new, positive activities that do not conflict with family rules. Having friends over or planning family outings can help teenagers rebalance their emotions and give them an alternative focus. Reinforce positive messages as much as possible.

Step 6: Be prepared to follow through

You will need to batten down the hatches and call in the support if you think you are facing a major battle. This is super-parent time! Be on guard to anticipate and respond to challenges. Once your teenager knows you are serious the fight is usually well on the way to being over. The first few challenges they send your way are the most critical. If you back down you will make it a lot harder for yourself next time. Bottom line — keep going once you have started.

What to do when nothing is working

I wish I had a magic wand to wave every time I have seen a loving parent lose their child to the tragic consequences of drugs or crime. For me there is nothing more heartbreaking to see a parent grieving over the self-destructive behaviour of their teenager. There are times when a parent has literally done everything possible, pulled out the reserves and given more, only to discover that things are spiralling out of control.

This is a desperate and very difficult place for a loving parent to be in. I have literally heard mothers and fathers both say, 'I had to pretend she was dead in order to cope. It was less painful to believe she was dead than to not know where she was or if she was safe.' This type of intense pressure and fear affects people in different ways. It is vital that parents realise that their health, their marriage, their career and other children in the family will all suffer it they don't keep a sense of focus on the broader picture. I have seen families lose everything under these circumstances.

I always encourage parents to judge themselves based on what they do, not on how their teenager responds. Blaming yourself for your teenager's choices is not going to help, nor will endlessly rehearsing your own faults. You have to know that you have done your best and remain secure in that.

I was recently part of a conversation between a 72-year-old man and the father of a teenage girl who had 'gone off the rails' and had just returned home. By 72 years of age people usually have something worth saying, so even though he was not a close friend of the father, we both stopped to listen to his opinion. The conversation went something like this …

'How's your daughter going?'

'Good,' answered the father. 'My daughter has settled down and moved back home. Things are 80% better and she has even paid us six weeks' worth of rent in advance. We are feeling positive things are moving in the right direction.'

'Now do you believe in yourself?' the old man asked insightfully.

'What do you mean by that?' probed the father wondering what he was getting at.

'She went through a tough time but you were there for her. Imagine how much worse it would have been for her if you hadn't stuck around. You thought you were bad parents but in fact you were perfect parents. You just lost your confidence. You should have believed in yourself as much as you do now things are going better.'

What simple uplifting advice. This guy should be hired as a parent coach!

Although there are no easy answers for parents in this situation, I have included a list of suggestions that may help provide some comfort that you are on the right track. I really hope this list doesn't sound trivial but provides a level of hope for the future.

Suggestion 1

Make a commitment to be there for your child, regardless. Commit to being her parents forever. This means the door of your heart will never be completely shut to her.

Suggestion 2

Realise that the parenting journey may be very long and difficult. Don't expect a quick fix but be prepared to appreciate each small step they take forward.

Suggestion 3

Distinguish between your life's journey and your teenager's life's journey. Although they overlap they also need to be separate. Define her choices and your choices clearly. Know what you can and can't control.

Suggestion 4

Know your limits and protect your health. No one is invincible and there is no shame in asking for help. Get support (or a team of support) to help you with parenting strategies and stress management. Don't neglect these things.

Suggestion 5

Protect other relationships in your life. Your marriage and other children are equally important and deserve your attention. Be very aware of neglecting them or allowing stress to dominate your relationship with them.

Suggestion 6

Try not to compare your teenager with other teenagers, or your family with other families. Comparisons will stop you embracing the value your own teenager has. Realise that each family's journey is different.

Suggestion 7

Keep holding onto the hope that the future will be better. The last chapter in your teenager's life is not written yet. Situations can quickly turn for the best and time can heal a great deal of wounds.

Chapter 6

I have nothing to wear

I want to feel beautiful

The ongoing quest for beauty

I love to watch parents in shopping centres handing over hard-earned cash to buy their daughter clothes. Some parents give a 'you'd better behave' lecture just before they commit to the purchase, others let out a huge sigh in protest as they reach for their credit card, while others nervously rummage through their wallet like they have been held hostage by a thief. However, there is one thing that unites them all. They all love their girls and want them to feel good about themselves.

There is a huge connection between your teenage daughter's appearance and how she feels. It is a connection that is complex and difficult to fully understand. Any parent who has waited in the car, ferociously beeping the horn while their daughter has changed into yet another outfit, knows this. Many teenage girls are compelled to pursue beauty.

The teenage years have a major impact on how we emerge as adults. And although I have no doubt the childhood years are the most influential, there is something powerful and pivotal that happens to a girl's self-image as she begins to grow into a woman. Each time she stands in front of the mirror, she is discovering herself. She is also making judgment about who she is.

Most women can recall the panic associated with getting ready to go out with friends during their teenage years. They recall the horrible uncertainty of not knowing whether an outfit was coordinated, of not knowing how to put on makeup, or of not knowing which way to wear their hair. We all have at least one dreadful photo of us as teenagers, looking like we were going to a Halloween party when it was actually Christmas! The worst part is that we thought we looked a million dollars!

When a teenager begins to get ready to go out, they have a vague idea of what they would like to look like at the end of the process. Obviously, they are on a quest to look beautiful. However, their concept of beauty is vastly different to that of most adults. A teenager's idea of beauty is usually based on a photograph of their favourite celebrity, which has involved specialised makeup, lighting, airbrushing and computer touch-ups. Teenage girls often attempt to morph their 13-year-old bodies into dynamic, sexy images they have seen on television.

The challenge for parents is that teenagers don't see glossy magazine images as fantasy. They have a strong emotional 'buy-in' to these images and really do believe they are attainable. This gives them a stereotypical image of beauty that is not based on real-life people or their poor parents' budgets! As a result, teenagers are often on a quest to find something very popular but not realistically attainable. It is an image that is advertised but unable to be purchased in their world. Most teenagers could spend all year getting ready and still not create the image they are hoping for.

This reality often hits a teenager just before they are ready to go out. They feel disappointed with how they look but don't know how to bridge the gap between what they see in the mirror and their expectations. It is not uncommon for teenagers to erupt in an emotional blow-out, crying, panicking and yelling during these times. They simply feel like they can't keep up with expectations and they put huge amounts of pressure on themselves to do so!

It is sad that so many girls feel like they can't measure up to these expectations. They often can't work out why they feel this way, because they are unable to make the connection between their unrealistic expectations and their feelings. Without knowing how else to handle their disappointment they conclude that they aren't pretty enough. Anyone looking on knows that this is far from the truth.

What is certain is that teenagers can't fully accept themselves and can't feel beautiful while they are comparing themselves to each other, or magazine photos or video clips.

Comparisons breed feelings of inadequacy, jealousy and insecurity. Most grown women will understand the lingering, nagging feelings of being 'less beautiful than models' or 'uncoordinated at organising a wardrobe'. Many of these feelings originated during their teenage years when they felt unable to compete.

It is very common for teenagers to define beauty as the one thing they can't have or be. For example, a girl who is short with dark hair may define beauty as being tall with blonde hair. Her definition of beauty may be based on a physical trait she admires in someone else but does not possess herself. I always ask teenagers to define beauty as something that they can realistically attain given their natural physical characteristics.

It is a huge challenge to help keep a teenager's concept of beauty realistic, balanced and undistorted, among all the pictures of perfection they are surrounded by. The teenage years are full of opportunities for girls to make harsh, illogical judgments about their appearance.

It is really disturbing to see a teenage girl unhappy with her appearance, especially when it begins to affect her ability to function in a healthy way and enjoy life. The irony is that it is often the most attractive girls who are the most self-conscious. They tend to isolate themselves and nervously fiddle with their hair. You can see their mind constantly thinking 'Do I look ok? Is anyone noticing my pimples? Do I look fat? Are people thinking my ears are too big?'

Nothing good comes out of a teenager feeling negative about herself. Eating disorders, shoplifting, alcohol abuse, drug use, depression and even suicide have all been linked to teenagers feeling unhappy with their appearance. Parents should keep a close eye on the intensity of their teenagers' negative feelings about themselves. Negative feelings have a tendency to gather momentum and quickly take over rational thinking.

We would all love to see our teenager accept and feel comfortable with both her physical strengths and weaknesses. There is nothing better than to hear a teenager who has a face full of pimples say that she likes her appearance. When a teenager can abandon her few physical imperfections in order to fully embrace her life she has found confidence. When she can hold her head up on a bad hair day, simply because she is comfortable with herself, it will have a positive impact on every area of her life.

It takes some girls longer than others to develop an appreciation for who they are. The best thing that parents can do is support this journey rather than fight it. Even if you do see it as being self-indulgent, try to be a positive part of the process. Recognise that through each dreaded trip to the shops they are building their self-image, layer by layer. It is a process that will take time and your patience. With the right support I'd hope the teenage years could be used to conquer their insecurities, rather than simply endure them.

Last year I purposefully brought a group of ten 14-year-old girls together. My aim was to gain a greater understanding of how they felt about their appearance. They were all beautiful to me, and had unique physical characteristics typical of their cultural backgrounds.

I planned for the discussion to last an hour but I found their enthusiasm for the topic meant they were happy to continue even after the school bell had rung. These girls had found a safe place to talk about the dominant issue in their lives — their appearance. I wished that their parents could have listened to the depth of thought that came from these girls. They would have been very proud of them.

I started by asking and explaining a pointed question, 'Who here feels comfortable with their appearance? By comfortable I mean reasonably happy with your appearance. You don't have to feel like you are the most gorgeous girl in the school. All I am asking is if you are comfortable with the way you look.' All I required was an anonymous yes or no response.

The girls nervously took a piece of paper to write their yes or no answer. As they wrote, I could see them guarding their answers with their lives. This was obviously an intensely private moment for many of them. They certainly didn't want *anyone* in the room to see what they had written, probably as they were in fear of being judged for their true thoughts. They covered their responses with their hands, folded their pieces of paper into tiny segments and handed them to me. I put them in a hat.

The big reveal began as I read out the answers. The girls sat on the edge of their seats eager to hear if they had answered similarly to the other girls in the room. When the final tally was counted, only four girls out of ten said that they were comfortable with their appearance. One at a time each girl began to voluntarily reveal the answer they had been previously hiding.

Although I had planned a discussion about perceived beauty and media images, these girls had far deeper ideas to bring to the table. My prepared notes were soon forgotten as the intense discussion about family values and its impact on a girl's ability to accept themselves took place. Although all of the girls recognised that media images drove teenage culture, they also believed that, on a fundamental level, their family's values overrode the impact of these images.

Parents — especially mums — should take special note at this point: the girls began to reveal their secrets.

In a heated discussion that followed, the girls conclusively decided that their mother was the most influential person in the development of their self-identity — the most influential person in their lives! (Who would have guessed?) The daughter who criticises how you dress each morning and refuses to walk down the road with you, actually thinks she is most likely to model her life on you. She recognises that you are the person she is most likely to 'catch' her value system from. No wonder she is so concerned with how you look — she thinks she is going to turn out just like you!

I was amazed how accurately these teenage girls were able to describe the personal struggles their mothers had with their appearance. The conclusion was inevitable. Mums, your daughters are watching you even when you think they aren't. They are watching how you judge yourself and whether you accept what you see in the mirror. They are not just watching your weight, but your attitude towards your weight. They are not just watching you lose weight, but they are watching how you lose weight.

The girls who were most comfortable with their appearance argued that their mothers accepted themselves, even though they weren't perfect looking. They believed that this helped them accept their own imperfections. They also believed it helped them value other qualities that made a women attractive, such as kindness.

At the end of the lesson I asked the girls to sum up what they had learnt about beauty. This is what they wrote.

> Other people say that beauty is a certain skin colour, very thin, perfect skin, long hair, tattoos, having a good-looking partner and sexy looking. We say that beauty comes from within, smile, not fake, just you, clean, being yourself and feeling comfortable, being your best and being successful at being you. Being comfortable with yourself means you aren't worried about what other people say, you aren't checking your hair all the time, you aren't always on a diet, you are happy with yourself, you don't cut yourself, you don't hurt yourself or damage your body.

I watched two girls in particular exit the room — Chelsey and Kim.

Chelsey was reasonably happy with her overweight figure. She was reasonably happy with the pimples on her face and the visible birthmark. She enjoyed life, had great friends and was confident choosing clothes. She accepted people for who they were rather than how they looked.

Kim was very unhappy with how she looked. She didn't like her salon-foiled hair. She didn't like her size 8 body and perfectly glowing skin. She had thought about plastic surgery more than once and she had even self-harmed because she hated her appearance.

Everyone has noticed the difference between teenagers who are comfortable and uncomfortable with their appearance. Being attractive is a lot more than beauty alone. There is nothing more unattractive than someone who thinks she is ugly. They are not pleasant to be around. Instilling confidence in our girls is worth investing a great deal of thought and attention. If you take their advice, the best investment any mum can provide is to accept herself first.

The impact of a mother

This letter below from Rachael, aged 14, was written after her mum had lost 20 kilograms. I asked her about the impact her mum's weight loss had had on her and this letter was a part of her response. She is a very eloquent and clever girl who really articulated what I think many mums would like their girls to understand about the reality of motherhood, life and appearance.

> Hey mum,
> Just recently I have started noticing how good you look and the way you look at yourself is improving heaps. Losing almost 20 kgs is an incredible effort and has made me so proud of you. It

has shown me that I shouldn't give up and that taking good care of my body is really important.

The last few years I have seen things get harder and harder for you. You were unhappy with your weight, with the way you looked and when you looked at yourself in the mirror you would say to me 'I look fat'. Watching you go through that was hard. It hurt to think that my mum, the most amazing mum in the world, would think like that about herself. Losing the weight has made you feel great, think great and when you look at yourself in the mirror, you no longer tell me how fat you are, you look great in what you wear and that makes me proud of you. It makes me sad to think that you had to go through the self-hating stage to come out on top.

As a mum, you put your children first. When we were younger and depended on you a lot more you would make sure that we were having the best chance at life. You took care of us and gave us the chance to be the best person that we could be. I guess that because you focused so much on us, you forgot to take care of yourself as well as you could have, and you put on lots of weight. I could see how much that hurt you. I could tell that sometimes you were embarrassed about your weight. You were so focused on us that you forgot about yourself.

Now that you have lost the weight you not only feel better about yourself but you get out with us all the time and we swim together, we go on walks together, we play at the beach and you get lots more involved with us than you could handle when you were overweight. It makes me happy when I can see how happy you are to be outside with us running around, even when you beat us at beach cricket!

I know that for me, watching you go through this has definitely inspired me to take care of myself and make sure I keep myself fit and healthy, whether that be playing sport, dancing, running, or just taking a half hour walk everyday.

Thanks mum! I love you heaps!

Rachael, aged 14

Boys and more boys

The following diary entry simply highlights the uphill battle many teenagers face when they are getting ready for school each day. I feel exhausted just reading this entry! With this dialogue going on inside of your head it is no wonder teenagers struggle to get ready in time to go to school!

Dear Diary

I'm holding in so much that I need to tell you. Everyone calls me pretty and beautiful. I want to have beautiful hair, face, body and personality. Every girl says how wonderful I am and how jealous they are, every guy calls me beautiful and hot but that's all on the outside. On the inside I'm feeling like crap. I feel fat and ugly. I feel so bad I cut myself to the extreme. How is that perfect?

My whole body is wrong. Every morning I get ready for war. I put loads of foundation, mascara, eyeliner and eye shadow on and of course straighten my hair but last of all before I leave the house I put a huge fat fake smile across my face! I hate everything about me so why are girls so jealous?

As a teenager I know that having the right amount of food for your body is necessary but I also know as a teenager it's very hard to eat right. I hardly ever eat as I always feel fat and if I do eat, I usually go straight to the bathroom to vomit it back up. Not eating makes me feel good as I feel skinnier and I am able to wear things that I like. Although I do all of this, I never actually feel quite skinny enough, like I could always lose a little bit more

> weight. I know not eating is wrong, but I would rather be skinny than fat.
>
> I hate this. I'm dying inside. I wish I could tell my mum and dad. I've tried but they just don't listen, they think I'm being stupid. It hurts so much to know that the only two people I care about the most don't even understand me. I'm so ugly, how could God make me look like this? I wish I looked like the models. They have a great life! Being so beautiful, why can't I be that great?
>
> **xx Laura, aged 15**

And why do teenagers feel like they have to look so impressive every single day of their lives? Anyone would think they were getting ready to meet the Queen! I asked a group of Year 8 girls this very question the other day and their answer was simple — *Boys!* Boys, I questioned? Surely those skinny, weedy looking Year 8 boys can't be the source of all this pressure! This was their raw response …

> Every day what I look like is commented on. The boys are obsessed with what girls look like, they especially like big boobs, which I don't have. Boys in Year 8 tell you exactly what they are thinking and all they are thinking about is sex. They only call you 'hot', 'sexy', 'babe', but when they call you beautiful you start to believe them and feel good about yourself. When you start dating a guy he is only using you for pleasure or hook-ups. They try to get you to do stuff with them when all you want is for them to spend time with you and like you for who you are not how you look. They say they have a boner when they look at you. This makes me

feel wanted and proud I am pretty and then freaked out at the same time. If they actually like you for who you are it makes you feel really special. When I do my makeup in the morning I think of who I am trying to impress. Most boys like what you have got not who you are. Before they judge you they judge your appearance. So if you look gross they call you a dog. So then we try to impress the guys and get them to say we look hot so we feel good. If you get noticed by a cool guy everyone likes you.

Boys in Year 8…

- *get jealous really easily*
- *touch their weeners (penis) in class*
- *they put their hands in their pants all the time*
- *get boners (erections) in class and tell everyone*
- *are obsessed with the size of their weener (penis)*
- *always ask your bra size*
- *always ask about your periods*
- *always ask to take pictures of your boobs*
- *ask if we are loose before they ask us out*
- *ask if we are frigid*
- *talk about our body to other people*
- *ask for hummers (oral sex)*
- *think it's a turn-off if a girl won't get fingered*
- *stare at your boobs.*

Unfortunately, it is my experience that this type of language (and behaviour) is quite common in high school. And even if your teenager is not boy crazy they have many girls around them who are. They are exposed to explicit conversations and imagery about sex, even if they are not directly involved in sexual activity.

It does greatly concern me to see many girls making sexual choices based on a desire for social ranking and approval. Many girls tell me that they love their boyfriend and that is why they are choosing to become sexually active. They often convince their parents of this too. A short time later (after they have broken up) they admit they felt pressured into being sexually active because they didn't want to look stupid or get rejected. They simply wanted to be accepted.

I don't intend to blame young men for the struggles many girls have with their appearance. However, I think it is important to acknowledge that their relationship with the opposite sex does shape a girl's self-identity. I think it is important for parents to truly understand the context that our girls are finding themselves in every day. There is a lot of pressure to look attractive to the opposite sex. Girls who do, get a lot more attention.

If parents can get their heads around the immaturity of teenage boy–girl relationships it will help them understand (and protect) their daughters. The bottom line is this: girls understand that being beautiful influences boys' opinions about them and, in turn, other girls' opinions about them. Their social ranking often has a direct correlation to how beautiful they are perceived to be by their friends. With this in mind, it is no wonder our teenage girls have such an emotional fit about getting ready each day.

So, what can parents do?

I do hear a few parents comment on their teenager's sexual activity by laughing it off and saying, 'They are going to do it anyway', or 'It is a natural part of growing up'. This is usually followed by allowing (or at the least tolerating) unsupervised time with boys. Unsupervised time can include sleep-overs, parties, hangout time and even day outings. (You would be surprised where teenagers have sex!) Some parents prefer to turn a blind eye and convince themselves it isn't happening. In turning a blind eye, unprotected sex can have a double-whammy effect on teenagers.

I recently counselled a family who had allowed their daughter's boyfriend to sleep over on the weekend. They had been going out for three months, which in teenage terms is almost marriage. He was actually a really nice young man who genuinely cared about their daughter. Her parents were totally shocked to find the contraceptive pill in the top drawer of her room. They had no idea their daughter was sexually active. She had told them they were only kissing and there was nothing else going on.

A few months later the teenage couple broke up, which had a dramatic effect on their daughter. A chain of rumours flooded around the school saying she was pregnant. At the same time she had some trouble with her regular friendship group and her best friend moved interstate. She quickly got another boyfriend, this time one who her parents definitely disapproved of. Things went from bad to worse, simply because the daughter didn't have the resources to handle a break-up on top of the normal teenage dramas she had to cope with. She sat in my office after having cut her arms several times in frustration with life.

I have rarely seen a teenage girl have the same boyfriend for longer than 12 months, no matter how in love they feel they are. And I have never seen a teenage girl's self-esteem strengthened after breaking up with a boy she was having sex with. In fact, I have seen quite the opposite. In my opinion, talking openly about the downside of boy–girl relationships in high school and discouraging sexual activity is sensible.

Parents may feel pressured to go with the flow of what is presented as modern culture. Your daughter may tell you that every other parent in the universe allows their daughter to have a boyfriend at 13! Yet if you feel your daughter doesn't yet have the maturity to handle the dangers and emotional impact of having a boyfriend, then why not say 'no' and apply sensible boundaries. She is only in junior high school and the shape of boy–girl relationships will change dramatically and be far safer as she gets older.

It is important for girls to understand that they are teaching the boys in their life how to treat them every day. They are teaching them what they will tolerate and what they will not. They are teaching them how they will be spoken to and what they will look at. I love seeing teenage girls confidently protecting their bodies and strongly setting their own boundaries. These girls usually have the boys in their lives on a string!

I would also like to highlight the importance of a father's role in his daughter's life. An active father (or father figure) can play a major role in building a teenage girl's self-identity.

Many girls I meet aren't lucky enough to have a strong male role model in their lives and I see those girls negatively impacted by this reality. They themselves often acknowledge they are looking for a father figure who will adore them.

I would really encourage dads to be a strong influence in their daughter's life and demonstrate to her how they should expect the opposite sex to treat her. I think that dads have a great opportunity to help their daughters understand boys and relationships. And although Year 8 boys are not likely to change in a hurry, they may realise that they have someone watching them who can beat them at their own game.

The beauty basics

When teenagers are unhappy, parents understandably look to give them more of what they want. They might take them shopping to buy them new clothes or the latest gadget, all of which can temporarily lift their mood and none of which is wrong. However, many times what they really need is routine and a boost to their general health. A teenage lifestyle can be very taxing on anyone's general health and wellbeing.

1. BEAUTY STARTS WITH GREAT HEALTH

The very first thing I do when mentoring a teenager is to ask her parents to give her body a full medical check-up. Growing up can put a great deal of stress on the physical body. Intense arguments with parents, sleepless nights worrying if their boyfriend is going to dump them and exams can all deplete the body. There is also the issue of hormones, mental health and the impact of any alcohol consumption.

To-do checklist

- Medical check-up: Consider asking for full blood tests and further investigation into hormone balance, viruses and sexually transmitted diseases if there are any concerns.
- Mental health check-up: For teenagers struggling with depression, anxiety, extreme anger, erratic behaviour, chronic sleeplessness or hyperactivity.
- Monitor the consumption of any recommended medication.

2. BEAUTY STARTS WITH GOOD NUTRITION

Teenagers rarely have a balanced diet, but it will help a great deal if you are able to model good eating habits and have fresh foods available when they are hungry. Try to eat one meal together as a family and provide them with lunch each day. Monitor your teenager's sugar consumption as much as possible, including chocolate and soft drink. Sugar consumption can dramatically affect mood. Remind them to drink plenty of water to help detoxify the body.

To-do checklist

- Monitor your teenager's diet and include fresh foods, lunch and plenty of water.
- Add vitamin supplements if their diet is inadequate.
- Model good eating habits.

- Try to eat one meal together as a family each day.
- Particularly watch excess sugar as it can destabilise mood.

3. BEAUTY STARTS WITH A HEALTHY LIFESTYLE AND EXERCISE

Exercise is just as important for teenagers as it is for adults. Because teenagers sit in school for six hours per day and are often glued to the computer when they get home, they can often be exercise deprived. Without planned exercise they can have a lifestyle that is as unhealthy as a desk-bound office job. There are many benefits of exercise, including a lift in mood and increased capacity to handle stress. When trying to add exercise into a teenager's schedule, work with their interests and consider enrolling them in a sport such as dance or netball.

To-do checklist

- Help them find an active interest.

4. BEAUTY STARTS WITH GOOD SLEEP

Teenagers love to push their bodies too far while enjoying sleep-overs, all-night movies and weekends that go, go, go! Although you can't stop this, remember to plan for down-time after the slumber parties are over. Teenagers need a lot of sleep. Sleep deprivation has a major impact on mood and a person's ability to cope with pressure.

To-do checklist

- Know how much sleep your teenager needs.
- Monitor their routine and allow for 'catch-up' time.

- Remember that an active, positive and healthy daily routine will help them sleep at night.
- Limit activities that stimulate the brain close to bedtime.
- Seek medical advice if your teenager has consistent sleep problems.

The art of shopping for teenagers

I simply can't finish this chapter without talking about shopping, the biggest social event on any teenager's calendar. Shopping is a huge part of many teenager's social lives, but it can be a huge point of frustration between parents and teenagers. This is usually because few teenagers know how to shop well, and poor shopping skills lead to a lot of wasted money.

This is how I think it goes for teenagers in many households …

> *Take a long shower, ignoring any thumps on the wall to speed it up!*
>
> *Put your favourite music on loudly.*
>
> *Make a commitment to look your best ever!*
>
> *Write in the fogged mirror — Cindy and Josh forever xx oo.*
>
> *Think about getting noticed by Josh if you look great.*
>
> *Dry yourself, add deodorant and moisturiser.*
>
> *Find all pimples.*
>
> *Squeeze them until you draw blood.*
>
> *Dry hair.*
>
> *Burn yourself a few times while hot ironing.*

Apply layers of foundation, black eyeliner and mascara.

If in doubt, add another layer of makeup.

Paint your fingernails black.

Choose something to wear, decide it makes you look fat … dump it on the floor.

Wish you had a figure like your best friend.

Choose something else to wear, decide the colour is wrong … dump it on the floor.

Wish you had better clothes.

Choose something else to wear, decide it looks silly … dump it on the floor.

Ask yourself, 'What will Georgia be wearing?'

Continue this process until the wardrobe is empty and there is a pile of clothes as high as Mount Everest on your floor.

Notice that all your fingernail polish is smudged!

Hear your parents calling HURRY UP! We are leaving!

Panic.

Remove smudged polish while panicking.

Check if you have enough eyeliner on.

Add some more just in case.

Throw some clothes on in frustration.

Where is my jewellery gone?

Leave your room like a bomb has hit it.

Come out of your room yelling, 'It's everyone else's fault I am late. I have nothing to wear! I need to buy some clothes. Take me SHOPPING!'

Mums and dads can often see the shopping experience quite differently. While many women relate to their teenager's feelings, dads are often left totally bewildered. They often feel like the third party, who hands out the cash, but has no real idea what is going on!

I recently talked to a mother about their daughter's shopping habits. She explained to me that her daughter felt she never had anything to wear, despite her mother taking her shopping continually. She explained to me that her husband regularly shakes his head in disbelief over the amount of clothes her daughter has. 'She has a pile of clothes on her bedroom floor the size of Mt Everest,' he says. 'Don't take her shopping again! Just tell her to find something she likes out of them! If I counted up how many wasted dollars she has lying on her floor we could all take a holiday.'

To hopefully avoid parents feeling this way about their daughter's behaviour here are some really practical things that parents can do to help their daughter shop smarter.

Shopping Tip 1: Get educated

Recognise that teenagers need to be taught how to organise and create a great wardrobe. It doesn't often happen naturally. If organising a wardrobe is not a skill you are confident with, involve another adult figure in the process. Consider a personal stylist, or a friend of the family acting as a stylist. A few hours with a professional stylist might be cheaper than endless unworn clothes. A stylist can also help your teenager become educated before she spends all your money!

Shopping Tip 2: De-clutter existing wardrobe

Start with organising her existing wardrobe. What does she wear and not wear? Which items don't have anything to match them? Which items are home clothes, casual clothes and good clothes? Take time to de-clutter the wardrobe each season and give unneeded clothes to charity. Don't let her clothes become one big pile that she can't manage.

Shopping Tip 3: Shop with a budget

Teenagers need to learn to shop within a budget. They also need to learn to make financial decisions and live with the consequences of those decisions. However, it is unfair for teenagers to be given a budget without a clear plan of how to establish a workable wardrobe with that budget. Without this they are most likely to randomly purchase items, run out of money and then still have nothing to wear.

Shopping Tip 4: Discuss fashion regularly

Encourage teenagers to read and talk about their body shape, favourite colours, makeup and anticipated prices of items before going to the shops. There are some great shopping magazines that can help teach teenagers the art of shopping and be a great point of discussion for mums and daughters.

Shopping Tip 5: Shop with a plan

Don't go shopping without a plan. Know what you are shopping for before you go, but be flexible when you get there. Remember that shopping is an experience of self-discovery that they should enjoy. Take into consideration these tips:

- Buy the basics first.
- Think outfits, not single items — go for a mix and match wardrobe.
- Finish off outfits with the right accessories (jewellery, handbags and shoes).
- Dress appropriately for the situation.
- Know the difference between attractive and immodest.
- Pick colours that suit you.
- Know what each item is worth — don't pay too much (use a budget).
- There is always tomorrow — if in doubt leave it in the store.

No one understands what I'm going through

I need help to deal with the pain

The period of reflection

It is not uncommon for teenage girls to become self-reflective and intense about the disappointments they have faced in their lives. Circumstances they simply accepted as a child may now feel complicated and confusing. Experiences such as a family break-up, abuse, or death of a loved one that they once approached in a carefree manner may now cause them a great deal of pain.

The primary reason for this shift is that teenagers process pain on an entirely different level than they did as children. Their developing cognitive functioning allows them to ask deeper questions such as 'Why do bad things happen?' and 'Why isn't life fair?' Hormonal changes can also play a role in intensifying their emotions, although parents should remember that physical imbalances are seldom the core reason for the problem.

Very few parents like to see their children suffer. I have heard many parents describe feelings of extreme helplessness as they watch their teenager struggle emotionally. It is an experience that parents understandably find impossible to separate their emotions from. As a result, it becomes a journey they need to travel through and find answers for together.

I know parents commonly wish they could turn back the clock and erase the circumstances that caused their daughters pain. However, no parents can give their child a perfect life free of disappointments or struggles. In fact, looking forward to the long-term results of such a pain-free environment would suggest it isn't beneficial at all. It simply wouldn't prepare them for the real world they will inevitably have to live in.

It is important for parents to realise that children can experience trauma and still develop into mature and functional adults. Painful experiences can be very valuable in a child's life. They can produce empathy, understanding, maturity and resilience. Nothing can replace the role of experience in a teenager's life and it is this experience that can give them an incredible advantage.

For all of us, pain can be productive. However, for every person there is a point where pain becomes crushing rather than productive. Parents should always be looking for signs that their teenager's pain is exceeding their resources for coping. General signs that a teenager is not coping well include mental instability (depression, anxiety, hearing voices), insomnia, loss of appetite, inability to socialise with others, abandonment of normal grooming, extreme or inappropriate aggression, headaches, stomach aches, extreme mood swings, isolation or unusually childish or immature behaviour.

If a teenager's pain is overwhelming her she will need both professional and personal support. Teenagers need their parents' help — not to take away the pain — but to help them accept and respond to it in a healthy way. Good coping skills, professional support networks and a healthy lifestyle are critical to ensure teenagers overcome life's challenges.

Facing family issues

I often ask teenagers to tell me about their greatest struggles in life. Almost all teenagers talk about family-related issues, no matter what situation they are in, even such as being expelled from school! I find that totally amazing! The family unit really is the centre of a teenager's world and what happens behind the closed doors of everyone's home does affect them. Here are a few of the letters I have received from teenagers explaining their greatest struggles.

> *Dear Michelle*
>
> *This is what it is like to have a dad who is kinda depressed. When your dad is kinda depressed he is always sad and he can get very angry very fast. He takes stuff out on you and also he acts weird. After a while he realises that he is making you sad and upset. He tries to make you feel better by buying you something but it doesn't really help. Mum and I*

talk about it all the time but she doesn't realise I am sad inside. When I am in bed sometimes I start to cry and wonder what could happen.

In the end I just stop crying and hope everything will be ok. I would like to talk to someone about what is going on because everyone thinks I am ok.

From Maddy (aged 15)

To Michelle

On Monday my mum told me that my dad had been having an affair with her friend for a year and a half. She told me that is the reason why she hates love so much. This got brought up because Dad has been showing that he loves his girlfriend more than me. I don't like her and neither does mum, so it all came out. My mum was broken, so was I. We had a fight before this so she turned to alcohol. She drinks a lot of alcohol when life gets tough. She got really drunk and because of this she told me everything.

My dad was living a double life with us and the other woman was oblivious to that fact. My mum was broken and shattered. The only people who know are my gran and me (dad doesn't know that I found out) he would be furious with my mum. Because of this I do not trust my dad anymore and I do not wanna be a part of his new life. I hate my dad's bimbo who doesn't care about others' feelings. My mum and I debate whether she has a brain or not. I feel second-best to her as he is on the phone for 4 hours a night and I spend that time in front of the TV. I found out about his engagement on Facebook.

I live with my dad more than my mum but after they get married I have a feeling I will move in with my mum instead. I have decided that I will put up with it as long as I can. But when it gets too much I am going to pack up all my stuff and go to mum's and never go back to dad's except for birthdays and special occasions. I don't ever want to get married. I hate love like mum.

Love Danielle (aged 16)

Dear Michelle

My parents getting divorced was really hard for me to deal with. It has affected my life in more ways than one. It tore my family apart and it never really healed. Both my parents are fighting over me all the time. One week I live with dad and then the next I live with mum. They disagree on everything each other is doing. My mum tells me to do something and then my dad says no. Then they end up fighting because they can't get their discipline right. Things always got physical. My parents took me to the doctor's and said I need help and then they sent me to a psychologist. I spoke to the lady for a bit and then she said she needs to speak to my parents because it seems as though they are the real problems!

From Ashlyn (aged 17)

Many of the disappointments teenagers experience within their family are genuine. It is no secret that every family has its own set of imperfections. Families can love each other dearly and still have difficulty solving problems together. Although family is meant to be a place of unity, stability, safety and refuge, there are times when it looks more like civil war. I think most families would agree.

It is unbearable for a parent to think that a broken relationship, a moment where they weren't supervising, a clashing personality trait, or a feeling their sibling was favoured, can cause their child pain. Issues such as stressed finances, affairs, violence, abuse of alcohol, lack of communication, drug use or mental health issues can have a big impact on a child, but it may not be until they are teenagers that they start to put all the pieces together and verbalise how they feel.

It is really difficult for parents to hear their children vocalise disappointments about their upbringing. It is especially hurtful when they are hurling their thoughts in a tone that is blaming, judging and lacking the maturity to see the full picture. When a teenager verbalises their disappointments, the most natural and instant reaction is to justify and protect your intentions, rather than listen. It takes great strength and security for parents to own their own inadequacies as human beings.

I really admire parents who can accept that, although they did their best, they weren't able to offer their children perfection. After all, that is the truth. When parents come from this viewpoint, not only can they apologise for the hurt they may have caused, they can begin to be a part of the process of healing. They can begin to help teach their teenager to make stronger choices in their future.

In order for teenagers to grow up they will need to work through the disappointments they have faced while living under your care. I know the thought of that is hurtful, but it is a real and necessary part of your teenager growing up. It is a process that parents should embrace and use to their teenager's advantage.

In my own work with Youth Excel's small group programs I use a reflection activity I find really helpful. It aims to help teenagers move from blaming their parents to accepting responsibility for their future. A key part of growing up is making choices about which parts of your childhood you want to leave behind and which parts you want to embrace and build upon. Most parents hope that their girls will be able to take the inadequacies of their family life and learn from them in order to create a future that is uniquely theirs.

To begin, I ask teenagers to complete a series of questions about their childhood. These are the type of questions they are already asking themselves while they are alone in their room at night. Once they have completed these questions we convert them into a statement. This statement identifies what they have learnt from their past and what they want their future to look like, showing them how to transition their disappointments into actions.

It is not uncommon for young people to become visibly emotional when writing their responses. Most teenagers know that their parents did their absolute best to love them. Writing about their hurts does not detract or take any of that love away. It does, however, give them the opportunity to acknowledge their feelings and take responsibility for how they will process them.

I have chosen to include Hannah's answers to this reflection activity and completed statement. Hannah was a middle-class 15-year-old girl I taught a few years ago. She has always stood out in my memory because she was so normal! Her story is a good example of the stories I hear. I hope that if your family is going through the same struggles you can identify with how this teenage girl needed to process the pain she was feeling.

My future: Questions and answers by Hannah

Question: Things I have seen in my life that I do want to be a part of my future ...
Answer: A nice house, financial security, good friends, family

Question: Things I have seen in my life that I don't want to be a part of my future ...
Answer: Adults hitting each other in front of kids, drinking too much alcohol, marriage in trouble, depression, not talking to your kids about divorce, threatening to leave all the time

Question: Things that are really important to me and I feel like I can't live without ...
Answer: Money and a house for my kids, husband who loves me, a family who gets along

Question: Mistakes I have seen adults make that I am determined not to make ...
Answer: Marrying the wrong person, fighting in front of kids, not being in love any more

Question: Good decisions I have seen adults make that I want to make ...
Answer: Getting an education, having a good job and providing for kids

Question: The type of adult I want to be ...
Answer: I want to be a good parent, not divorced, someone who is loving, someone who is responsible and doesn't walk out and leave for no good reason

My future: Statement by Hannah

My name is Hannah and I am absolutely sure that I don't want divorce to be a part of my future. I don't want to marry the wrong person or be unhappy in love. I want to have a happy family that I want to come home to.

I would like to leave behind physical violence and aggression. I believe that each person needs to be treated with respect. I don't ever want to hit my kids in anger. I don't want to see people physically hurting themselves due to depression. Relationships are precious and I never want to take people for granted.

It is really important that I have a good relationship with my family in the future. I need to take responsibility to communicate well with people that I love and work out my problems. I need to take responsibility to apologise for what I do wrong and forgive.

I have seen adults make the mistake of drinking alcohol too much and too often to wash away their problems. I have seen adults buy things to try to make them happy and then get into debt. These are things I would like to leave behind as I grow into an adult.

I don't want to lose my parents' trust but always have a close relationship with them. I want my parents to be a part of my future. I want kids. I want to marry someone who loves me for who I am.

I would like to be a successful person who has enough money to care for my family. I see myself as a happy, smart, successful and loving adult.

Breaking a barrier

Some time ago I sat with 17-year-old Jess. Jess was in every way communicating that she wasn't coping with life. She believed that no one understood what she was going through and that no one could help her. Both her parents were desperately trying to understand what was wrong with their daughter. Why was she so unhappy all the time? Why did she constantly push them away? Was this just normal teenage behaviour? Were her hormones imbalanced or was there something else going on they didn't know about?

I had come from a business appointment that day so I had on high heels and was carrying a diary. Under normal circumstances this teenager would never relate to me. But that day Jess and I had an incredible time together. The more she spoke the more comfortable she became. About halfway through the conversation I could feel the door of her heart swing open. It was her moment to share a very private and personal secret.

'Can I tell you something that I haven't told anyone else? Can you promise you won't say anything to anyone? Can you promise you won't tell my parents?'

This is a line I have heard so many times before. My heart sinks when I hear it because I know what is coming next. I can almost guess the exact words that I am about to be told.

'That is a hard thing to promise Jess. I rarely would need to tell your parents. I'd think you would be mature enough to speak to them yourself if you needed to.'

'So you won't tell them?' she asked hopefully.

'I can't absolutely promise but, let's put it this way, I don't think I am going to need to.'

I could see her fidgeting. The tough exterior she was carrying began to melt away.

'Well. When I was 14 I was raped by a guy. He was heaps older and I didn't know him. We were hanging out in a vacant land block away from all our other friends. He was just there with his friends. My parents didn't know I was there. I know I shouldn't have been there.'

'Did you want to tell them?' I asked.

'Yeah, but it was my fault. I shouldn't have been there.'

'Have you ever thought about telling them?'

'Yeah heaps of times. When I get really angry I think about telling them but then I get scared. Then it all goes away again.'

'How much are you thinking about it?'

'All the time. I can't get it out of my head.'

'Do you think telling your parents would help them understand what is going on with your emotions?'

'Yes, but I am really scared to talk to them. Dad will hit the roof and I don't want mum to cry and cry. I have already messed things up enough. I feel like I have wrecked their life.'

'Secrets create invisible walls between two people. They are like a barrier that no matter how hard people try they can't get through. You might have noticed it has been more difficult to relate to your parents since it happened?'

'It's like I try to talk to them but they never understand me. I'd like it to be different and I know mum would, but I don't know how.'

'How about we talk about different options you could take from this point on? It is your story. You can choose if, when and how you tell them.'

Jess ended up choosing to talk to her parents about the incident and a few other horrible experiences she'd had. I sat with them as the truth came out, offering my support to both Jess and her mum and dad. Dad didn't hit the roof. He did extremely well at supporting his daughter. And mum — she did cry (what mum wouldn't), but after some tears and questions she was really able to look forward and be a part of the answer. They all hugged for the first time in three years.

Finding out your daughter has been abused can be very traumatic for parents. There are a range of questions they ask themselves: 'Why didn't I see it? Why didn't she say something? Why didn't I protect her?' When a child is abused, a parent is also abused. Any type of child abuse is an abuse of a parent's love and protection of a child.

Jess's honesty was difficult for her parents but it did bring a lot of hope into their relationship. Although things weren't instantly fixed, both mum and dad could be more proactive and a part of the solution. They knew what they were dealing with and, like great parents, they wanted to deal with it together with their daughter.

I have often wondered why teenagers speak about such personal issues to me. What I have realised is that teenagers do genuinely want to talk to their parents and I am often the next best thing. I think subconsciously they often want me to tell their parents for them so they don't have to face the shame they feel revealing the truth. Teenagers genuinely worry about their parents' ability to cope, just as much as parents worry about their teenager's ability to cope!

The impact of abuse

Abuse is especially difficult to deal with if the abuser has been a family member. I feel very privileged to have been given the following impact statements, written by a teenager who was the victim of sexual abuse and her mother. These statements were used in a recent court hearing against the criminal actions committed by the teenager's Poppy (grandfather).

Although the following impact statements are heart wrenching to read, I have included them because I know families who are in a similar situation will identify with them. I also know that these impact statements will reinforce to all families the importance of protecting their daughter against sexual predators. I greatly appreciate this family's contribution and their willingness to use their own experiences to help others.

The following statements were written at the very beginning of this family's journey towards healing. Since this time all members of their family have been able to move forward and rebuild those areas that were understandably devastated. They are a perfect example of how people of all ages can find incredible strength in bonding together in order to overcome life's darkest challenges.

Cassey's impact statement

> My name is Cassey and I am at present 14 years of age. I would like to share with you some of the effects the crime that was committed against me has impacted on my life.
>
> I have lost trust in people, I think people are only nice to me because they want to get something from me. This is very hard for me. This reflects on how I have not many friends.
>
> I am filled with guilt and shame. I feel this is my fault and that I have ruined my mum's family.

I feel dirty and disgusted in myself and of what was done to me. I self-harm myself to try and get rid of this feeling.

I have nightmares constantly that he is coming to get me and of things that were done. It is like reliving it over and over again.

I am always thinking he is there somewhere watching me and I have become very paranoid.

I lose concentration all the time because thoughts about him get into my head, this is affecting me in everything I do.

I have lost Poppy, Grandma and Lucky, the dog I loved, all because of what he did.

Poppy was the most special person to me and we shared some good times, now I am lonely and I don't have that anymore.

My mum's mother died when she was 11-years-old, she only had her dad, now because of all this she has no one and I feel responsible for that.

What has happened has impacted severely on mum and my relationship. We fight all the time, I don't tell her anything because I think she will harm someone or herself if someone hurts me again. This has made her severely protective of me.

Mum doesn't like to let me stay over people's houses or to go many places as she is untrusting of everyone now.

My eldest brother has turned to drugs and has caused hell in our house because he can't handle what's happened. My other brother is in denial about it all.

My mother is broken, she is no longer the fun sparkly person she was. She doesn't leave the house very much anymore and never wants to go anywhere.

My mum is filled with guilt because the person she trusted most in her life betrayed her. This person hurt one of her children and she didn't know and she thinks she should have known.

She thinks this is her fault because she used to let me stay over and spend time there.

I was Poppy's favourite girl and now I know it was for all the wrong reasons. I feel used and betrayed.

There are so many more fights in our house. Our once happy place is now very close to a hellhole. No one is the same.

This will live with me for the rest of my life. I cannot change what happened to me and I know that I am not to blame, but knowing this isn't any help to me, because of all the guilt, shame and hurt.

I am extremely angry all of the time. I have this rage that eats at me every day. I go to a counsellor to try and help with this.

I have wanted to die lots of times. I have hurt myself a lot of times. I am also seeing the counsellor for this.

At the end of the day this has affected my life now and forever, it has altered the person who I am and has changed my whole family. Nothing can fix this.

I haven't told my mum a lot of things that had happened, because I don't think she will cope with them. This makes it hard for us to talk about things.

Natasha's impact statement (Cassey's mother)

My name is Natasha. I am a mother of four children. I have three boys and one girl. I am married to a great man.
I would like to tell you about the impact this crime has had on myself and my entire family. I will try and be as brief as possible. Writing this is an extremely hard thing for me to do, but I will do my best.

The impact that has affected myself and family are as follows:
I am Natasha only by name, because anyone that knows me knows the person I once was, I am no longer. I have become

withdrawn. I trust no one, absolutely no one. I am extremely angry, filled with a rage that is slowly eating away at me.

I have let my daughter down. I didn't protect her.

I have been betrayed and used by someone that I loved and trusted.

My children all suffered in different ways. My eldest son could not cope with this and turned to drugs and alcohol. My second son — he is just not facing it so he is in denial, my youngest just doesn't understand as he is too young. My husband wanted to kill my father. He has resentment towards himself for not seeing anything.

My marriage is in serious trouble, the constant fighting, the mood swings by me.

I don't sleep very much.

I dream constantly about trying to save my daughter.

I feel cheated.

I feel like this is all something that I should have been able to see but didn't.

I had to tell my sisters and ruin their lives also. I have such guilt about this.

Cassey and I don't talk very much as she doesn't want to tell me things because she is scared I will hurt people if they upset her or hurt her.

He built a relationship up with Cassey just so he could manipulate her, told her that we didn't love her and that he was the only one that did. This isn't something that can be easily fixed. Cassey thinks because she told me about Poppy it is her fault that he is going to jail. She doesn't fully understand that he is going to jail because he committed a crime. She thinks that because she took the money and gifts from him that it is her fault. Deep down I think she blames me for me telling the police. It was my only option and this in turn has sent her Poppy to jail. How do we get past this?

I am lost and I just don't know where to find that piece that seems to be missing.

This has altered everything in my life for now and for the future. My kids are sick of me being overprotective and want me to lay off.

I am no longer living, I am just existing and I hate this feeling of all these mixed emotions that whirl around in my head.

I feel very insecure and lonely. I feel like I am in mourning, like my father died, then something happens and it starts all over again.

Cassey is not allowed to stay over at friends. This causes lots of fights. I stand up for Cassey even if she is in the wrong because I don't want to ever let her down again.

I do things to try and make myself feel better, like shopping but only maxed out the credit card. This only made me feel worse. I have let myself go in appearance having to really push myself to make an effort. I have to make myself get out of bed every day otherwise I would just stay there.

I want this nightmare to never have happened. But we live in reality and that is not going to happen. I want to live again and be rid of this guilt and sadness.

Things parents can do

You may not be facing the impact of sexual abuse in your home. However, any type of abuse impacts upon family relationships in a similar way. You may relate to aspects of Cassey and her mother's impact statements even if you are in an entirely different situation. The abuse of trust, power, drugs, alcohol, money, or physical strength has a ripple effect throughout the whole family.

I often hear parents describe the feeling of having lost contact with their daughter. Others say they feel like they are relating to an entirely different person. Most don't know what to do to return things to their previous state and begin to realise that abuse can have an ongoing effect that is not limited to the incident or a defined period of time after the incident.

Most teenagers have to deal with some form of trauma at least once in their teenage years. Some of these situations may be extreme, while others have the potential to have an extreme effect if left unattended. I always encourage parents to be proactive and act quickly rather than wait until the problem is out of control. Teenagers are rarely able to process pain well without support.

For this reason I have included an overview of the different support services available to parents and teenagers dealing with trauma. Please access them, understanding that it is very difficult for families to handle these type of challenges without support. Each service is slightly different and therefore has a different set of skills to offer your family. There is no reason why a number of these services can't be used at the same time.

Doctors (General Practitioners – GPs)

Doctors are often underestimated for their ability to support families during times of stress. Look for family-oriented GPs who have an interest in teenage health. Some GPs are also counsellors and advertise this additional qualification. Some clinics also offer a range of specialists for families.

Psychologists

Psychologists are highly trained mental health professionals legally required to register with the Psychology Board of Australia in the same way medical practitioners must be registered. Some psychologists specialise in counselling and life coaching. You do not need a referral from a doctor to see a psychologist, although your local GP may be able to suggest one in your area. The Australian Psychological Society also provides a national 'find a psychologist' service on their website (www.psychology.org.au). Rebates are available for selected psychological services under both private health funds and Medicare. Psychologists work with a wide range of people and problems so it may take time to find one who relates well to teenagers. However, once you find one who is a good fit for your daughter they will be an invaluable support. Although they are not able to prescribe medication they will be able to provide appropriate counselling, therapy, and self-help support and also assess if your daughter has any serious mental health concerns that require referral to a psychiatrist.

Psychiatrists

A doctor can provide a referral to a psychiatrist. A psychiatrist is ideal for a teenager who is struggling with serious mental health issues that require medication. In many cases, both a psychiatrist and a psychologist may work together to provide comprehensive treatment and support. Again, an initial appointment to assess their suitability for your daughter is recommended.

Counsellors

Counsellors hold a variety of qualifications and levels of experience. They all have their own fields of interest and expertise. You may have to shop around until you find the right person for your daughter. Before sending a teenager to a counsellor I always book an appointment with them first. This appointment gives me an opportunity to interview them and assess if they are the right fit for my client. I suggest you do the same for your daughter.

Life coaches

Life coaches offer a proactive approach that can be a very good fit for most teenagers and their families. Much like counsellors, life coaches hold a variety of qualifications and levels of experience. Always thoroughly check a life coach's qualifications before utilising their services.

School support staff

Guidance officers, school counsellors and chaplains are just some of the people your teenager may relate to at school every day. School support staff can be an invaluable support to families. Parents should try to keep in regular contact with school staff as they hear more about your teenager than you do.

Teachers, mentors or coaches

The influence of a coach or teacher outside of school can be invaluable. Again, there are plenty of options, so don't feel limited to theatre, dance, netball, tennis, swimming or art. Keep your eye out for programs and mentoring opportunities in any area that may interest your teenager. There is always a range of sports, social or cultural groups that teenagers can become a part of after school hours.

Church-based youth leaders

Church youth groups can provide great social and spiritual programs for teenagers. There are many types of programs available, including weekend and holiday programs. Contact your local church for details on what they offer.

Youth workers

Check out your local newspaper or contact your local member for information about community-organised holiday or mentoring programs for teenagers. There are often some great programs available free of charge to families.

Chapter 8

It's all your fault

I know I can't blame you

The blame game

Emma is almost 14 years old. She is the daughter of successful businessman, Peter, and primary school teacher, Celine. They are an educated middle-class family. Emma is well dressed and well spoken. She attends a private school and in all respects has a stable life to come home to. Emma, however, is going through a difficult patch and has experienced a few of life's hiccups in recent months.

I asked Emma to write a letter to her parents explaining how she was feeling about her current relationship with them. The result was surprising to say the least! If I were to read this letter without knowing Emma's parents, I would think that Emma was a neglected and misunderstood child.

However, knowing the inside scoop, nothing could be further from the truth. Her parents adored her and were spending every waking minute attending to her. Emma's letter is a perfect example of a young lady who is ferociously saying, 'It's all your fault' when her parents clearly had no intention of harming her.

> *Dear mum and dad*
>
> *This is what goes on in my life! You are going to hear me out and you are really going to listen instead of telling me to stop being stupid and acting like a b****!*
>
> *OK. So my ex-BFF (Grace) is a backstabbing b****. I told her my secret and now she's gone and told everyone! My BFF (Savvy) is leaving me now. I HATE Chantelle! I don't know if Indi likes me.*
>
> *My friend who is rich I invited her to my house, and she said, 'Is this it then? Bit small don't you think!' I am mad at you for not listening and not caring. I need glasses but you are ignoring me. I can't see the whiteboard and it's all fuzzy. I get headaches when I read. I feel ugly all the time cause you don't believe in me. I act all grown up but I'm still a little girl who needs her mummy. OMG! I can't believe I said that! You are so emotional that even dad can't relate to you. Then you are so non-emotional when I need you! What hope do I have? And on the subject of my father ... Why haven't you been my father? You are always working, who would know if you were really working or having an affair? Maybe you are! You disgust me! If you were there none of this would happen. And one more thing: You have moved me away from everything that I know. ALL my friends. You say it is going to be better for us but you don't really care what I think. You don't speak to me about it so how can you know that it is better for me. You are always working. Because you*

ignore me, I feel stuck in a hole. I see the light but no matter how far I run I never get there. It is like I am on a treadmill. I am running but I am not getting anywhere. I went through depression and you treat me like a piece of s***. You never listen. You even left the room once when I was trying to talk to you. You just don't want to know about stuff that is important to me and all you care about is yourself. It is all your fault that everything is like this. If you weren't bad my life would be ok!

Emma, aged 13 (almost 14)

The truth is that teenagers are so busy blaming everyone else that they fail to see their own faults or realise their own responsibilities. It is far easier for them to draw attention to their parents' weaknesses than deal with their own. Parents can be bending over backwards, putting up with hell on earth and crying themselves to sleep at night, but in their teenager's eyes it still isn't enough. If teenagers can convince their parents that they are the ones to blame, it provides a plausible excuse for their actions.

Teenagers might sound like raving lunatics but they are, in fact, very calculated. They know exactly how to tap into their parents' weaknesses in order to get their own way. In fact, they often use their parents' weaknesses like a dagger. They take their parents' biggest shortfalls and highlight them in bold letters. They wave them around mercilessly until their parents feel overwhelmed with inadequacy. Teenagers are very, very good at throwing blame at parents when they are, in fact, in the wrong themselves.

I can't recall the amount of times I have heard teenagers directly blame their parents or teachers for their own poor choices. I personally find it difficult to comprehend how teenagers can truly believe they aren't responsible for any of their actions. However, over time I have come to accept the fact that I can't convince them otherwise. It is a genuine blind spot!

Most parents try to defend themselves to their teenage daughters by explaining the restrictions of an adult world and the pain and suffering they too are experiencing. They try to convince their teenager that their thinking is selfish and wrong, which usually starts a whole heap of more fighting. Parents believe that their teenager should be able to see logic if they just listen to the other side of the story. They become very disappointed when their teenager doesn't care about the other side of the story!

The three journal entries that follow are written by teenage girls who participated in one of my small group programs this year. They were all struggling to stay engaged at school and had very legitimate challenges in their lives. However, when it came down to the bottom line question, 'Who is responsible for your actions?' they unanimously decided it wasn't them. These journal entries are a perfect example of how most teenage girls think!

> *Everything (and I mean EVERYTHING) that happens to me at school is a teacher's fault. When a teacher tells me to stop talking it is the way they say stop talking that makes me really mad. They use their power against you. Today Mr Haylan told me to stop talking and I said, 'In a minute'. He started yelling at me so I started yelling back. He was the*

one who started yelling, not me. He is always the one who starts it and then I get into trouble for just defending myself! I have to stick up for what is right. He just wouldn't shut up even when I told him he was making me angry!

Anna, aged 15

My sister is the stupidest f***** b*** around. She is in fact my half sister and not my full sister and she comes and stays every second weekend and I hate it when she comes. She touches my stuff and then I yell at her and slam her. If she didn't touch my stuff she wouldn't get slammed. It's simple! Touch my stuff and I punch your head in! My mum comes and says, 'Stop hitting your sister!' But I just say p*** off because what does she expect! I say, you should be yelling at her not me! I haven't done anything wrong!

Erin, aged 16

It's not my fault I am in trouble all the time. My mum just lets me. I asked her if I could go to Dreamworld and she said, 'I have had three phone calls from the school this week so you can't go.' I said, 'Please you have to let me go. You are going to ruin my social life.' She says no. I keep going on and on until she makes me promise to stop smoking. She says I can only go if I start treating her better. I feel bad because I never do any of my promises but she always lets me go in the end. I am the boss really and I just make her feel guilty and keep promising until she lets me go.

Sinead, age 14

I find that many, many parents secretly search their souls to consider if they are the ones to blame for their teenager's bad behaviour. This response in itself is responsible and appropriate. However, taken to the extreme, a parent who internalises the thought that it is 'all their fault' finds that their confidence is quickly undermined. A parent who is always second-guessing their decisions lacks the authority they need to do their job well. It is difficult to parent confidently out of a mindset that says, 'I should have' and 'I could have.'

Teenagers very easily turn legitimate issues, like family problems or incidents of abuse, into an excuse for rebellious behaviour. In doing so, they can make their parents feel incredibly guilty. When parents feel guilty, they lose their confidence. Parents then find it difficult to discipline the bad behaviour they feel responsible for. Instead of allowing their teenager to feel the consequences of their actions they begin to shelter them.

The number one thing that stands in the way of good parenting is plain old-fashioned guilt. This guilt is often stirred up by their teenager's accusations. When parents carry guilt it limits their ability to make logical decisions that are best for their daughter. They feel compelled to consider everything from their teenager's perspective. If a teenager can blame you for their poor choices they cripple their parents' decision-making processes and, in turn, gain a license to behave in any way they choose.

Parents have a choice as to whether they buy into this blame game or not. They have the opportunity to step back and realise what is going on before getting emotionally trapped. They can either crumble under the pressure and bury themselves in guilt or stay dedicated to doing the best job that they can. Parents need to realise that their confidence will be tested by their teenager. It is a parent's job to stand their ground. This decision has a huge impact on a parent's capacity to parent.

The great assumption

The great assumption is that if you are a really good parent, and make the 'right' decisions, your children will sail through their teen years into adulthood without a hiccup … or a jail sentence. We would all love to believe that successful parents always produce successful children. However, in reality it isn't always that simple. Your teenager's behaviour is not always a reflection of you.

You can be the best parent in the world and your children can still go through difficulties in their teenage years and beyond. There isn't always someone to blame. There isn't always a grave error in your parenting style. When it comes to parenting, 2 + 2 doesn't always = 4. And there is definitely no magic formula. No one's journey is the same.

Mothers, in particular, need to take note here.

Most mothers I meet carry a virtual list of their failings as they would carry a handbag. It is imprinted on their memory just like their credit card's PIN and they don't go out without it. They hang on to their inadequacies and rehearse them regularly, just in case they forget that they aren't perfect. Even small inadequacies can bother mothers. I hear confessions such as, 'I never finished my child's baby album', 'I spent more time with my first child', 'I didn't make my child do their homework in primary school' and 'I forgot to dress them in free dress on the last day of year 3'!

Mothers usually try to blame every one of their child's bad behaviours on their own inadequacies. That can make them very good at excusing their teenager's bad behaviour!

Whenever I have an appointment with a mother I always allow time for her to go through her 'I am an inadequate mother list' first. I don't usually have to ask her to recite it. It is often the first thing she wants to get off her chest. She wants to make sure that she isn't as bad a parent as she feels she is and that her choices haven't resulted in the mess she sees in front of her.

There are often legitimate shortfalls on the part of parents. Parents needn't run away from those. No parents should be aiming for perfection. You have to aim to do the very best with what you have to face right now, remembering that your best may be very different to the parent who lives next door. My philosophy is this. If you have done your best your teenager will eventually believe that this was enough, regardless of your shortcomings.

Parenting can't be copied off someone else or compared to someone else. It is unique to you. Although you may be able to glean from others' insights, it has to come out of your own expression of love for your child. It is dependent on everything unique about you and your child. It is two people's journey through life together.

All parents have strengths. One parent may value self-discipline, academic performance, opportunity and financial provision. Another parent may value relationship, acceptance, self-expression and creativity. Some may argue that they simply want to get their teenager through to adulthood alive! It would be unrealistic to be everything your child needs. You have to be comfortable providing what best suits your set of skills and attributes as a parent.

Despite what teenagers say, they don't need to know you are perfect in order to believe that you love them. I always like to ask parents who are in doubt themselves this question, 'Is your motive love?' If the answer is yes, there is a great possibility you are giving it all you have. The intent with which you parent will speak volumes to your child in the years to come.

Many teenagers have unrealistic expectations of their parents. Many parents have unrealistic expectations of themselves. Unrealistic expectations mean you will never be good enough and this allows room for teenagers to load guilt on you. I recommend parents release themselves by releasing the expectations. That means that there are no superhuman parents, just ordinary ones like you.

Take the 'I am the perfect parent' off this year's new year's resolutions. In my opinion you are far better off saying, 'Yes you are right. I am not perfect. I make mistakes but I am still your parent and I am going to do the best job I can.'

Buying into the blame game

Yes, I admit it. I was eavesdropping! It was about 10 am and I was waiting for a Deputy Principal who was running late for his appointment with me. I had been given a seat in the hallway and while I was attempting to read a book I overheard a guidance officer and a mother having a heated discussion. Their office door was open, and my seat was a few metres away ... so what did they expect! I tried not to listen, but my curiosity just got the better of me. It was far more exciting than the book I was trying to read!

Sally had been suspended for seven days for swearing at a teacher and leaving the school grounds. The incident had started when Sally didn't bring her homework or books to class, once again. In the heat of the moment Sally apparently swore at her maths teacher, jumped the school fence and walked home.

The guidance office was firmly explaining to her mother that Sally was not the type of student that the school was looking for. She simply did not fit the criteria and, as a result, she was coming very close to being expelled. Her mother was attempting to defend Sally's behaviour. She was trying very hard to find a legitimate excuse for Sally's actions. I am sure Sally's mum thought she sounded logical at the time. However, from where I sat it sounded more like Sally's mum had been conned into participating in the blame game.

Here is how the conversation went.

'I believe my daughter. If she says she didn't swear at the teacher then she didn't swear at the teacher.'

'I assure you that Mr Kenneth wouldn't make up stories about Sally. This is very common behaviour for Sally,' explained the guidance officer.

'That is my point exactly. You are looking for trouble from her. She doesn't even have to do anything wrong to get in trouble anymore. She just turns up to class and they throw her out. She is really trying. I have seen her attitude change at home but no one in this school wants to give her a go. Mr Kenneth sounds like an unreasonable teacher.'

'I assure you that Mr Kenneth is a fine teacher. Sally hasn't even been bringing books to class and she refuses to write anything or participate. We can not tolerate that type of behaviour at this school.'

The guidance officer was starting to lose her patience.' I want her removed from his class immediately,' demanded Sally's mother.

'There isn't an alterative class for her to go to. We have already been through this. She was already taken out of Mrs Meed's class and she can't return there,' explained the guidance officer.

'Anything would be better than Mr Kenneth! I want you to know that I am not going to allow her to be picked on. I will make sure she gets treated with respect here. I will not tolerate …'

Unfortunately, the deputy was ready to see me and I had to leave the eavesdropping to the numerous others who had by then joined me! (Shame — I wanted to stick my head around the corner and add my unsought opinion: 'Excuse me mum,' I would have begun. 'My name is Michelle and I have never met your daughter. I know nothing about her. I do, however, know that she has sucked you into the teenage blame game.')

Like you, I hear teenagers complain about their teachers all the time. It is their favourite topic to whinge about. There are times when I am tempted to agree and admit that school rules are restricting and don't always cater for individuals. However, whenever a teenager tells me, 'My maths teacher hates me. As soon as I walk into the room he automatically tells me to get out even if I am doing nothing wrong!' I hear alarm bells. If it doesn't sound right, it usually isn't right.

I know it goes against all natural parenting instincts to allow your child to be punished, particularly when parents have always rescued their children from potential danger. One of the greatest skills a parent can ever learn is how to protect a teenager without rescuing them from the lessons they need to learn in life. Being overprotective is not about having too many rules, it is about protecting teenagers from the consequences of breaking the rules. Parents can't afford to be overprotective.

Please don't defend or excuse your daughter the first time she leaves the school grounds, let alone the one hundredth! Teenagers need to know that boundaries are fixed. They stand regardless of the circumstances that surround them. They are not open to negotiation or compromise. Teenagers need to understand that growing up means they make and live with their own choices. They are choosing consequences for their lives not just behaviours.

I searched high and low over my years mentoring teenage girls to see if I could find one who would admit responsibility for their own poor choices. No such luck! Instead I found a consistent barrage of blame from teenagers of all social classes, all ages and all cultural backgrounds. They blamed their teachers. They blamed their parents. They blamed their siblings. They blamed their peers. They blamed anyone that moved!

I also found that their parents were secretly trapped under this blame. On the outside those parents looked like they were in control and had it all together. Behind closed doors they greatly doubted their parenting. Most parents smile in public and put their best foot forward. You might think they are handling life with ease, but you don't get to see what goes on behind closed doors. Because of this, many parents assume they are the only ones who are struggling with knowing how to handle their daughter.

This book has so far focused on secrets that teenagers won't tell their parents. I would like to take a minute to share with you secrets that other parents may not tell you. If parents were to be really honest, they would tell you that they all struggle. In fact, the greatest secret I can share with you is that parents, in general, lack confidence in their skills, even the really good ones.

I try to go out of my way to speak to parents whose teenagers did not leave home under good circumstances. These are the ones I want advice from as they have the most experience of the challenging side of teenagers. I ask them to tell me their whole story, including the bits they usually leave out. Most parents oblige, but I can see it is really uncomfortable for them to talk about their fears, regrets and disappointments. I like to think of this information as their family secrets and treat it this way.

These are the wise words of Wayne, and his wife Lilly. I know them to be very dedicated parents of three children. Two of their children breezed through their teenager years and are now responsible adults. Their youngest daughter took a different path in life and at 18 is still finding her feet. I asked them to share their thoughts and experiences with me. I want to thank them so much for their honesty and time.

Here is the interview I had with them.

What is your experience of parenting a teenager?

I can only talk about our situation with our youngest daughter. Our other two were easy to bring up. There were a series of things that contributed to the problem, but bottom line she just had to learn the hard way. She bucked against us the whole way and made choices that really worried us. The biggest concern for us was the amount of alcohol she was drinking. She would turn into a completely different person. We couldn't believe she would be so stupid.

We would see glimmers of hope and then she would start hanging around the wrong crowd again. I think it was the people she chose to hang around that influenced her the most. We called them her loser friends because that is how we feel about them. It wasn't the way we brought her up to behave and she knew better. She would come home and say, 'At least I am not doing drugs like this person,' or 'You think I am bad! You should see what that person does.' She would compare herself to the wrong crowd. They were all unemployed and doing drugs.

Since your daughter has left home has your relationship with her improved?

Yes. We asked her to leave home when she was 18 because she couldn't comply with the rules of our house. This was actually the hardest decision we ever made, but the best thing we ever did. We are hopeful that she will continue to grow up and our relationship with her will improve. It is 70% better than it was, and she is still only 18 with a lot of growing up ahead of her. We are hopeful that one day she will love us as much as we love her! Teenagers don't understand what their parents go through. They don't even understand what their siblings go through. They are selfish.

There is still some tension though. When I ask what she has been up to she gets quite defensive. She thinks I am prying into her life. She says, 'If you are going to start on me then I won't talk to you at all.' There is nothing I can do but back off. It is her way of controlling the conversation. I am looking forward to that day when things are free and we can talk like adults.

Looking back, is there anything you would do differently?

I would be much stronger from the beginning. I am honestly sure of this. I would not deviate at all. I would not give any room for compromise. I would do this very, very quickly and not allow things to get off track. I should have been stronger when it first started happening. I let her get away with too much and before I realised it I had lost control.

I was scared of losing my relationship with my daughter. That is why I gave in to her too much. I call it feeding the beast. Teenagers can sense it if they can get around you. I thought I was doing the right thing by compromising. It was too late when I realised that I wasn't actually compromising. I was actually being manipulated. I was being played. By then I was in the habit of negotiating everything with her. She was always negotiating her to advantage.

Wayne, what was your greatest struggle?

I blamed myself too much for her behaviour. I would always ask myself, 'Where have I gone wrong?' and 'What can I do to turn things around?' I still find myself asking whether it was my fault. I believe it was the feeling of guilt that trapped me into making many other mistakes.

I thought if I took the time to talk to her about her feelings she would trust and respect me. Now I know she was using that as a way to manipulate me and get what she wanted. She was happy when she got what she wanted. It had nothing to do with whether our relationship was good or she felt trusted.

I listened to what she had to say too much. I know now that she was very clever at blaming me for her behaviour. She was very good at using my weaknesses as a parent as a way of deflecting her behaviour. She would always say, 'You never let me do this' or 'You are always acting like you don't trust me.' It made me feel that maybe I needed to trust her more.

I felt guilty. She was very good at using my weaknesses against me. She would say things that made me question myself. I think the arguing was the thing that wore me down the most. It was relentless and I thought I was doing the right thing by talking everything through with her. I have learnt that you can never win an argument with a teenager. Even if you think you have won you find out later you were outsmarted.

Did it affect your marriage?

Absolutely it did. It put a big pressure not only on our marriage but our whole family. I often chose to give in to our daughter because there were other children in the house that were being affected. You don't want your other children to be affected by the arguments. You worry about them too. It tears a parent up to choose between family members.

I would give, give and give and nothing seemed to make her care about us. I would feel like a cash cow that handed out the money to keep the peace. I felt manipulated into giving her money when I knew I shouldn't. She did nothing around the house and my wife wouldn't want to come home to the tension so she would stay out. I had to realise that the other people in my life were just as important to protect.

Lilly, what was your greatest struggle?

What wore me down the most was worry. I would worry about where she was and what she was doing. I couldn't go to sleep at night if she wasn't home. I would read things on Facebook that were written as a joke, but I would wonder if they were true. Sometime I said, 'I don't want to know.' It was just too painful to know. The worry that mothers carry is exhausting for them. It is a constant worry that doesn't leave them.

What else was going on in her life at the time?

At one stage she lost her job, and it affected her confidence a lot. We were very conscious of this. She didn't really understand what happened and I don't think it was her fault. It was then that we started feeling sorry for her and possibly giving her more trust to boost her confidence. I wouldn't allow this to cloud our judgment next time. Her job, confidence, choice of friends and behaviour were related. However, feeling sorry for her didn't help things.

How is this generation different to your generation?

When I was a teenager, my father would tell me to do the dishes once and I would do it. We had a fear and a respect for authority and we didn't speak back or argue. You just did what you were told. I guess I expected parenting to be more like that. These days teenagers fight back until they get their own way. They wear you down and I wasn't prepared for that.

What advice would you give parents?

Be strong from the beginning and don't back down. I honestly wish I had been stronger. That is my only regret. I had to live with that regret everyday.

My guess is that every parent holds secret pains in their heart with regard to their parenting. Most parents I speak to have regrets and fears that they hold close to their heart and haven't been able to fully share with others. Hearing these secrets, and being heard, can greatly help parents normalise their feelings of inadequacy. They can also help parents accept their own journey with their teenager, whatever that journey may be, knowing that others experience the same struggles.

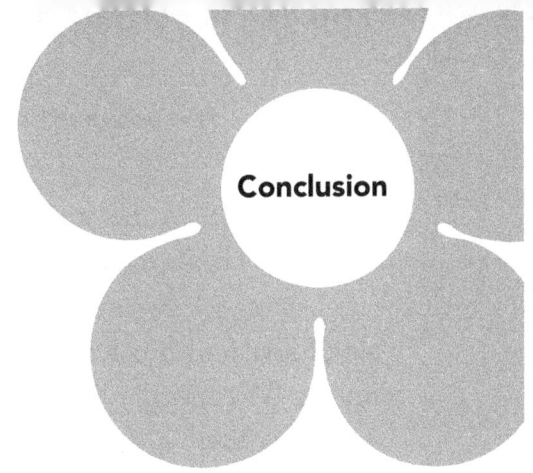

Conclusion

Looking ahead

Let's conclude this book by fast-forwarding life about ten years. Your teenager is now in her mid-twenties and I can guarantee that she will have well and truly left behind her schoolgirl mentality. She will have made decisions about her future based on the reality of her own life experiences, rather than childish ideals. She will be turning into a young woman.

This may feel like a long way off, but time will pass quickly with a mark of maturity coming each and every year. Your teenager will very soon be an adult with an entirely different perspective on life. It will only be then that they will tell you secrets like, 'I didn't really hate you', 'I just wanted to be accepted,' 'I did smoke that bong behind the school shed,' and 'Thank you for protecting me against myself!'

I absolutely love seeing teenagers transition into adults. I think I love it so much because it is often a healing time for families. The relationship that many mothers have secretly wished to have with their teenager often begins to take form. It is a great delight to hear parents say, 'It was so nice she asked our opinion!' It is also great to hear parents and teenagers laugh about the most difficult moments they faced together.

Because I love seeing this transition so much, I collect 'I am sorry letters' from troubled teenagers who are starting to grow up. A few years ago I met a 22-year-old who had written her mother a beautiful 'I am sorry' letter. This girl had spent some of her teenage years away from home, living at friends' places and was a perfect example of a teenager who was saying 'I hate you' with all of her might. I keep a copy of this letter in the drawer of my office desk. I regularly pull it out for parents who are in the thick of the battle to read.

I would like to share this letter with you and hope it leaves you with some encouragement for the future.

> *Dear mum,*
>
> *I don't know where to begin to say that I am sorry for everything I have put you through. I know I have said I am sorry a hundred times before (and sound like a broken record) but I truly am. I feel so bad thinking about all the things I said and did to hurt you. No matter what our differences are there is*

Conclusion

nothing better than having you in my life. Mum, I don't think I would have survived or have even been alive today without you. You are the only one who stood by me when my friends had gone. I know you spent so many nights awake, imagining horrible things were happening to me, and wondering what went wrong. I don't know what I was thinking. I'd like to call that stage in my life my crazy stage and put it behind me. All I could think of was what I wanted to do and how much happier I would be if I could run my own life. I was overly emotional and almost all the time had no idea why I was doing what I was doing.

I want you to know that you are the best mum in the world. I know that there is nothing you won't do for me. I can only hope that I can be as good a parent as you have been to me. I want you to know that I am changing and things are going to be different. I have already quit smoking and you know that I haven't touched drugs for ages. I am working on getting a job so I can take care of myself. I want you to be proud of me. Mum today is your birthday and I want you to be happy. I don't ever want to be the person who makes you unhappy anymore. I love you so much and I just want to say thank you for standing by me.

Love always.

From your daughter Kelly, aged 22

To me this letter puts into words what every parent needs to hear. It provides the validation and understanding that every parent deserves. Parents who commit to parenting regardless of its challenges usually end up being greatly respected by their grown-up children. Once their daughters gain an adult perspective they can't believe how their parents 'put up with them' and demonstrated such faithfulness, endurance and patience.

There is a good chance you will be on the receiving end of a letter like this one day. (Bring on that day I hear you say!) Hopefully that day will be sooner than later, and it will fill your life with the joy of knowing you have come out 'the other side' of parenting a teenager. In the meantime, I encourage you to hang in there and keep reminding yourself that there will be light on the other side of the challenges you are currently facing. You can only hope that your example inspires them to do the same with their own daughters!

notes

notes

notes

notes

notes

notes

notes

notes

www.ingramcontent.com/pod-product-compliance
Lightning Source LLC
Chambersburg PA
CBHW032254150426
43195CB00008BA/452